CONTENTS

Foreword by Cardinal Dziwisz 7

How 2 Use This Book 9

Preface 15

Introduction 19

33 Considerations to Help Us Learn
   Something about Love 39

    1. Is Love Possible? 41
    2. Do You Love? 45
    3. Dare to Love 49
    4. Lessons of Love 51
    5. Language of Love 57
    6. The Great Commandment 64
    7. Father of Love 68
    8. Word of Love 71
    9. Fire of Love 76
   10. Gift and Mystery 80
   11. The Greatest Mystery 83
   12. God Is Love 87
   13. Who Is My Neighbor? 93
   14. Eros and Agape 99
   15. Forgiveness 106
   16. As I Have Loved You 113
   17. If You Love Me 117
   18. Wound of Love 120
   19. Destined to Love 125

20. One Flesh 130
21. Crucified Love................................... 135
22. Mother of Love.................................. 143
23. Communion of Love 150
24. School of Love 157
25. The Great JPII 162
26. Love's Great Lovers........................... 173
27. Love Your Enemies............................ 183
28. Social Doctrine of Love 186
29. Civilization of Love 192
30. Till the End of Time 200
31. Love Alone.. 205
32. The Victory of Love........................... 209
33. To the End 215

Conclusion................................... 223

Love Zone — An Anthology of Love 227

Fr. Stan Fortuna, C.F.R.

Our Sunday Visitor Publishing Division
Our Sunday Visitor, Inc.
Huntington, Indiana 46750

Nihil Obstat:
Msgr. Michael Heintz, Ph.D.
Censor Librorum

Imprimatur:
✠ John M. D'Arcy
Bishop of Fort Wayne-South Bend
November 11, 2009

The *Nihil Obstsat* and *Imprimatur* are declarations that a work is free from doctrinal or moral error. It is not implied that those who have granted the *Nihil Obstat* and *Imprimatur* agree with the contents, opinions, or statements expressed.

The Scripture citations contained in this work are taken from the *Catholic Edition of the Revised Standard Version of the Bible* (RSV), copyright © 1965 and 1966 by the Division of Christian Education of the National Council of the Churches of Christ in the United States of America. Used by permission. All rights reserved.

Excerpts from the *Catechism of the Catholic Church, Second Edition*, for use in the United States of America, copyright © 1994 and 1997, United States Catholic Conference — Libreria Editrice Vaticana. Used by permission. All rights reserved.

All quoted material from Pope John Paul II and Pope Benedict XVI copyright © Libreria Editrice Vaticana. Used by permission. All rights reserved.

Excerpts from the English translation of the Non-Biblical Readings from *The Liturgy of the Hours* on pages 64 and 76-77 copyright © 1974, International Committee on English in the Liturgy, Inc. All rights reserved.

Every reasonable effort has been made to determine copyright holders of excerpted materials and to secure permissions as needed. If any copyrighted materials have been inadvertently used in this work without proper credit being given in one form or another, please notify Our Sunday Visitor in writing so that future printings of this work may be corrected accordingly.

ISBN 978-1-59276-337-5 (Inventory No. T436)
LCCN: 2009940312

Interior design by M. Urgo
Cover design by Amanda Miller
Cover and interior photos by Dominick Petrungaro

PRINTED IN THE UNITED STATES OF AMERICA

Love is something that cannot be taught,
but it is absolutely valuable
that we learn something about it.

— *Karol Wojtyla/Pope John Paul II*

FOREWORD

Love was the dominant force in the life of our beloved Holy Father Pope John Paul II. *U Got 2 Love* is a practical and well-documented presentation of the gift and mystery of this love. It's like a little school of love.

Fr. Stan's evident love for and devotion to John Paul II and his wonderful successor, Benedict XVI, makes this book useful in helping us continue the great legacy of love Pope John Paul II left for the Church and the world, especially for the young.

May all who read and reread this book be inspired to pass on the fire of this love heart to heart, more and more, every day. John Paul said, "Man cannot live without love" (*Redemptor Hominis* #10). Take this book and set the world on fire with love!

Cardinal Stanislaw Dziwisz
Personal Secretary to Pope John Paul II

How 2 Use This Book

How to use this book? Use this book over and over and over. Many of the texts contained in this book are intended for us to continue to read and re-read in order to soak in the light and love from many people who have been inspired by God to help us grow into the fullness of true love for service to the common good. Growin more and more into the fullness of this love, with greater service to the common good, is extremely necessary in the face of the great challenges of the new millennium — that's why we got 2 love. A greater effective connection and communion with this love is necessary for us to face these great challenges with a global culture of solidarity, for the buildin of the civilization of love. On September 7, 2002, the great Pope John Paul II said the following regarding the terrorist attacks of 9/11/2001:

> The reprehensible terrorist attacks of 11 September last, and the many preoccupying situations of injustice throughout the world, remind us that the Millennium just begun presents great challenges. It calls for a resolute and uncompromising commitment on

the part of individuals, peoples and nations to defend the inalienable rights and dignity of every member of the human family. At the same time, it demands the building of a global culture of solidarity which will find expression not simply in terms of more effective economic or political organization but more importantly in a spirit of mutual respect and cooperation in the service of the common good.

By receivin more love, we can become ready and willin to live more love, so true love can increase more of the time, and eventually and hopefully develop into all of the time includin the many ways and times we don't even see what's goin on, so that love would have us start all over again makin a new beginnin. This is crucial for fruitful and effective service to the common good. Yes, love can even have us be content with this dynamic of the love that never ends and always has more to give. Moreover, love can have us even come to love this never endin overwhelmin energy and movement of love that keeps us goin, perseverin to the end with the love that goes to the end, that never fails, and picks us up to begin again when we do fall and fail. Amazin …

As in my previous two books, *U Got 2 Believe*, and *U Got 2 Pray*, the linguistic style of this book includes contemporary phrases of urban slang in both content and "spellin." Please know that this is the intention of me the author, and not the result of poor copy editin on part of the publisher! It's all me! Sometimes I like to write like I talk so this can be more of a talkin book even though you're readin it!

The human person is understood in a more complete way in the sphere of culture.

Man is understood in a more complete way when he is situated within the sphere of culture through his language,

*history and the position he takes toward the fundamental
events of life, such as birth, love, work and death.*

— JPII, *Centesimus Annus* #24

In his message for World Mission Sunday, the great Pope John Paul II said, "A new apostolic outreach is needed ... taking into account each person's needs in regard to their sensitivity and language." I'm hopin the language and style of this book will reach out to your heart and commitment to the critical and burnin need for love. I pray through the intercession of the great Pope John Paul II (JPII) and Blessed Pope John XXIII (J23), who was beatified by JPII on Sunday September 3, 2000, for a "breath of newness" not only for the all important and necessary doctrine and content in this book on love but also for its style, presentation, and the way the content and doctrine are explained and expressed. At the beatification Mass, Pope John Paul II said the followin about Blessed Pope John XXIII: "The breath of newness he brought certainly did not concern doctrine, but rather the way to explain it; his style of speaking and acting was new." JPII and Blessed J23, please help all who encounter this book to have a new and fresh encounter with Love.

St. Paul preached the Gospel in a language that was understandable.

*After preaching in a number of places, St. Paul arrived in
Athens, where he went to the Areopagus and proclaimed
the Gospel in language appropriate to and understandable
in those surroundings (cf. Acts 17:22-31). At that time the
Areopagus represented the cultural center of the learned
people of Athens, and today it can be taken as a symbol of the
new sectors in which the Gospel must be proclaimed.*

— JPII, *Mission of the Redeemer* #37C

This book can also be used to help us befriend some of the great lovers of God so we can become better lovers ourselves, reformed and renewed in the radical newness of the new order of love. To help make progress in achievin this end, we have the "Love Zone — An Anthology of Love" at the end of the book with all kinds of stuff about love and related to love from all kinds of people. Check out Blessed J23 reachin out in love to the great lover of God St. Philip Neri:

> *St. Philip [Neri] is one of the saints most familiar to me ... O my good father Philip, you understand me even if I do not put my thoughts into words. Time is drawing on; where is that faithful copy of you I was to have made of myself?... O teach me the principles of your mystical school, for the education of the soul, so that I may profit by them: humility and love. I need great concentration of mind, Blessed Philip, pure and holy gaiety and enthusiasm for great works. (Blessed Pope John XXIII)*

Another way to use this book is to pray — pray before you read it, pray while you're readin it, and pray after you read it. Here we go — let us pray:

O God, put in my heart a hunger for greatness in all that I do. Give me the lovin heart of a generous servant. Protect me from being attracted to anything that can produce attitudes of arrogance and superiority, whether it be in Church or community, school, or business, or among family and friends. Show me how to humble myself out of love for You. Captivate me with Your Love and the joy of bein lifted up by You — the amazin experience of bein exalted through the Mystery and extravagance of Your Love. Increase within me faith, hope, and the greatest of all love. Let the demands of love become familiar to me, and the power of love reign in me as a major source of inspiration. May love be the dominant force in my life. Let the all-powerful combo of humility and love break down all traces of pride and self-seekin, producin within me an abundance of joy and enthusiasm for great works flowin from the greatest of all gifts, the gift of love, through an ever increasing and generous gift of myself. Amen.

Welcome the love of Jesus and allow yourself to be drawn to Him and respond to such love.

Jesus said, "When I am lifted up from the earth, I will draw all men to myself" (Jn 12:23). The response the Lord ardently desires of us is above all that we welcome His love and allow ourselves to be drawn to Him. Accepting His love, however, is not enough. We need to respond to such love and devote ourselves to communicating it to others. Christ "draws me to Himself" in order to unite Himself to me, so that I learn to love the brothers with His own love.

— Pope Benedict XVI, Lent 2007

As the great Pope John Paul II declared in his message for World Mission Day, May 18, 2002,

Only God's love, capable of making the men and women of every race and culture into brothers and sisters, can make painful divisions, ideological contrasts, economic disparities and the violent abuses that still oppress mankind disappear.

PREFACE

My favorite poem from the great Karol Wojtyla — the great Pope John Paul II — is "*To Milosc mi Wszystoko Wyjasnila*" (It Is Love Which Has Explained Everything to Me). So far I have never seen it translated into English. It was given to me durin one of my many — thanks be to God — visits to Poland and translated by some fine Polish friends. *It Is Love Which Has Explained Everything To Me*. That's it! Just the title of the poem says it all. He also said, "Love is something that cannot be taught, but it is absolutely valuable that we learn something about it." So I hope and pray this book helps us learn somethin about love.

In order to love, you got to know yourself as bein loved, and the moment you encounter the event that makes you know that you are loved, the beginnin is born that has no end. The possibility of the reality of us actually bein happy becomes real. Our awareness of this dynamic of love caries us to the end and helps us to carry one another through everythin that can happen to us. This connection with Love is difficult; actually it's impossible, especially in the midst of so much brokenness, weakness, and sin. Our connection with Love becomes impoverished resultin in us settlin for and engagin in a love that is impoverished. Yet, in spite of this real and diminishing possibility, the gift and reality of Love that is unearned and undeserved, the connection with the event that gives rise to the certainty of us comin to know ourselves as bein definitively and infinitely loved patiently waits for us. This connection unleashes a youthfulness that unceasingly provides the inspiration and energy required for us to go out of and beyond ourselves into the richness and fullness of Love. That's why we got 2 love; we got 2 love in light of the absolute value of us learnin somethin about it.

We see the reality of this great truth of love in great saints and heroes — those known and unknown — as well as in every person who strives to become and is en route to becomin saints and heroes themselves. My great hero, and one day (4 sure) to be proclaimed great pope, saint, and doctor of the Church, the great Pope John Paul II, said, "To be young means living within oneself an incessant newness of spirit nourishing a continual quest for good, releasing an impulse to change always for the better, realizing a persevering determination of dedication" (November 15, 1978). All youthfulness has its origin in God, and God is love. So it is love that keeps our hearts young with a youthfulness that never ends, that can understand as well as "stand under" the reality of the demands and delights of the reckless love that is necessary for total self-givin. This youthfulness created and sustained by Love will help us to enrich all forms and expressions of impoverished love. This will help us to be more and more disposed to have love explain everything to us. As the great Pope John Paul II said in his next to last book, *Rise Let Us Be on Our Way*, "It takes a young heart to understand the reckless love necessary for total self giving." May the greatness of the example of his life and death — his person, priesthood, pontificate, and patrimony, his words and his powerful intercession help keep our hearts young with love; may he help us find ways every day to have love become the dominant force in our lives, so we too can have love explain everythin to us.

U got 2 love? Yes. Sometimes we could have the feelin that it's impossible to live love because love has lost its power. Don't let that stop you. I hope this book will be a help for you and me to learn somethin about love, to provide motives for generosity and courage in pursuin and accomplishin the tasks and demands of Love.

Love always brings victory and is never defeated.

Sometimes one could have the feeling that before the experiences of history and before concrete situations, love has lost its power, and that it is impossible to practice it. And, yet, in the long run, love always brings victory, love is never defeated.

— Pope John Paul II, Ireland, 1979

Don't worry if you feel a little discouraged because of impoverished love in your life, in your culture, in the lives of others, with everybody everywhere. The Love that we got 2 love made himself very small and accessible one silent night in Bethlehem. This "smallifyin" of Love appeared in order to take away our fear of the greatness of Love, as well as our fear of the greatness of our vocation to love with the love with which we have been loved. Ultimately we got 2 love because Love wants nothin other from us than our love, "through which we spontaneously learn to enter into his feelings, his thoughts, and his will. We learn to live with him and practice the humility of renunciation that belongs to the very essence of love" (Pope Benedict XVI, Christmas Eve, 2006). So let's "small ourselves up" as we continue to learn somethin about love. The good news is that learnin somethin about love never ends — just like the Love that goes to the end and carries us all along the way.

Let's pray: I pray for you and me with the words of and through the intercession of my hero and mentor the great Pope John Paul II, and Mary Mother of God/Mother of Love: "Help us have a big heart that is able to understand love and give itself, that is not frightened either by evil nor by error; that embraces courageously its brothers and sisters and works totally in charity." Amen.

INTRODUCTION

There is a frantic call to chaos shriekin in our blood and in the blood of the cultures that shape the reality of our lives as we know them. This blood is cryin out for love as the broken heart of the world is pumpin its terminally infected blood through the veins and into the body and soul of the cultures of our world. One of my beloved mentors and heroes, Abraham Joshua Heschel (from now on respectfully with love and affection AJH), cries out with prophetic passion that this is no time for neutrality (a position of disengagement, to withdraw, to release from something that engages):

> *One of the lessons we have derived from the events of our time is that we cannot dwell at ease under the sun of our civilization, that man is the least harmless of all beings. We feel how every minute in our civilization is packed*

with tension like the interlude between lightning and thunder. Man has not advanced very far from the coast of chaos. It took only one storm to throw him back into the sinister. If culture is to survive, it is in need of defenses all along the shore. A frantic call to chaos shrieks in our blood. Many of us are too susceptible to it to ignore it forever. Where is the power that could offset the effect of that alluring call? How are we going to keep the demonic forces under control? This is the decision which we have to make: whether our life is to be a pursuit of pleasure or an engagement for service. The world cannot remain a vacuum. Unless we make it an altar to God, it is invaded by demons. This is no time for neutrality.

I hope we hear the distinct voice and feel the passionate love of this great man — 4 sure this is no time for neutrality in the midst of such a frantic and destructive allurin call that is effectively impoverishin love in global proportions. AJH also raises a great question: "Where is the power that could offset the effect of that alluring call?" To allure means to entice by charm or attraction or fascination, to attract artfully by arousing desire. Well, right out the box, as you might imagine, I'm makin the claim and stakin my life on it that this power is love. More specifically, I'm talkin about what the great JPII has taught us, not only with his great teachings, but most especially with the greater heroic witness of his life and death — that great heroic witness he gave to the reality of the power given to the human person to participate in the very same love with which God loves us.

I dedicate this book to the great JPII, who suffered and succeeded to make Love the dominant force in his life. I also entrust the usefulness of this book to his intercession to help us bear abundant fruit that will last (cf. Jn 15:16). Pope Benedict XVI (B16), while preachin at the amazin grace-bestowin event of JPII's funeral, amazingly revealed that JPII was able "to bear a burden which transcends merely human abilities." This ability on the part of JPII to bear a burden which transcends merely human abilities happened because JPII continually found ways to make Love the dominant force in his life with a burnin and impassioned love for Jesus. His communion with Love was so real that "tirelessly and with renewed intensity" he proclaimed the Gospel, the new order of love, the mystery of that love which goes "*to the end*" (Jn 13:1). Durin JPII's great funeral, B16, quotin JPII, referred to the new meaning of sufferin that Jesus achieved, openin it up to a new dimension and a new order — *the order of love*. B16 continued, "He interpreted for us the paschal mystery as a mystery of divine mercy." JPII concluded in his last book that "the limit imposed upon evil is ultimately Divine Mercy" (*Memory and Identity*, pp. 60-61). In addition, B16 made the following conclusion while he was reflectin on the failed attempt to assassinate JPII: "In sacrificing himself for us all, Christ gave a new meaning to suffering, opening up a new dimension, a new order: the order of love. Impelled by this vision, the Pope suffered and lived in communion with Christ, and that is why the message of his suffering and his silence proved so eloquent and so fruitful."

ſufferin burns and consumes evil with the flame of love.

It is this suffering which burns and consumes evil with the flame of love and draws forth even from sin a greater flowering of good.

— B16, quotin JPII at his funeral, April 8, 2005

It's this new order of love that can empower us to reverse values in our lives that need to be turned around by overcomin evil with good, which in turn will help us to establish and keep love as the dominant force in our lives. It's the unchangin nature of Love that is the one and only reality that can make us and keep us real. The fact that we don't always pull off livin this power of love faithfully is one thing, but the fact that this love "never fails" (1 Cor 13:8) is everything. The vocation to love and suffer with this kind of love is the key. JPII singled out love as bein "the fundamental and innate vocation of every human being" (*Familiaris Consortio* #11). As B16 points out, it's a part of every human love that it is only truly great and enrichin if, when, and to the degree I am ready to deny myself — to give of myself and drop the question, "What do I get out of it?" It's through this logic of love that life attains its greatness, enrichin human love with Divine power, with the Love that "never fails" and goes "to the end."

---

*D*rop the question.

Christ once said: "Anyone who wants to save his life will lose it," and only the person who loses his life, who is ready to give it up, can manage to see things in true perspective and will thus find his life. That means in the end I just have to drop the question as to what I get out of it. I have to be ready to give myself. I have to learn that it is important to just let myself go.... A part of every human love is that it is only truly great and enriching if I am ready to deny myself, to give of myself. And that is certainly true of our relationship with God, out of which, in the end, all our other relationships must grow.... With this attitude I no longer ask what can I get for myself, but I simply let myself be guided by him, truly lose myself in Christ.... When I abandon myself, let go of myself, then I see, yes, life is right at last, because otherwise I am far too narrow for myself. When, so to speak, I go outside, then it truly begins, then life attains its greatness.

— Pope Benedict XVI, *God and the World*, p. 44

Love can gap distances created by our inadequacies, weaknesses, limitations, and everything else that causes separation, includin the ultimate separation as a result of death. If absence makes the heart grow fonder, presence makes the heart new. This newness causes a kind of explosion, breakin and shatterin into pieces all concern and fear of bein broken and shattered. From this multiplicity of complexities is born the simplicity of love, which releases the capacity within us for love to become more of a dominant force. This simplicity of love is hidden from the learned and the clever (cf. Mt 11:25), and becomes manifest as Divine Love paradoxically bestows the capacity for union through its extreme humility in us small and unfinished souls.

Only love can expand my heart.

Because I was little and weak he instructed me in the things of love. There are the secrets hidden from the learned, and to possess them one had to be poor in spirit.... The yoke of the Lord is sweet and light; it is only love that can expand my heart.

— St. Thérèse of Lisieux

It's the work of Love that mysteriously brings about the possibility of union through the revelation of a communion that is unknowingly already present. It's kinda like goin east to go west, north to go south, up to go down, while the sense of direction pales by virtue of bein carried along by Love. That's the union, the majestic communion that's buried and waitin to be unleashed in each person. Each person is yearnin for this communion and in need of that intimate explosion of goodness which is unceasingly triggered by Christ crucified — his dyin on the Cross and risin from the dead — the event and energy of the Paschal Mystery.

Only a profound explosion of goodness can change the world.

Jesus makes himself our travel companion in the Eucharist, and in the Eucharist … effects a "nuclear fission" in the depths of our being. Only this profound explosion of goodness that overcomes evil can give life to the other transformations necessary to change the world.

— B16, August 24, 2005, General Audience

This event is itself a Person; Jesus is God, and God is Love. This great Mystery of Love penetratin the deepest stream of history, includin the smallest and biggest details of our lives, could not have happened without his birth, which could not have happened without his Mother Mary — Mother of Love. This is Love at work equippin us for the work of love — the emptyin of ourselves so we can be so filled with love. This gift and movement of Love will help us progress along the path of makin a more complete gift of ourselves; for it is love alone that will secure our happiness in this life and in the life to come.

Mary shares in the shockin mystery of the Cross.

At the foot of the Cross, Mary shares through faith in the shocking mystery of this self-emptying. This is perhaps the deepest "kenosis" of faith in human history. Through faith the Mother shares in the death of her Son, in his redeeming death; but in contrast with the faith of the disciples who fled, hers was far more enlightened. On Golgotha, Jesus through the Cross definitively confirmed that he was the "sign of contradiction" foretold by Simeon. At the same time, there were also fulfilled on Golgotha the words which Simeon had addressed to Mary, "and a sword will pierce through your own soul."

— JPII, *Mother of the Redeemer* #18

Love Alone

Love alone is the power that can deter and conquer the unceasin and ever more popularized and "mainstreamed" effect of that frantic and destructive allurin call which impoverishes love. Love makes us *"more than conquerors"* (Rom 8:37). Love's abidin mysterious presence which "endures all things" instills a confidence in our hearts that is the fruit of humble trust. This humble trust turns to dust the power of pride which prevents love's abidin abundance and ever-expandin extravagance to have us remain in the love that shields and heals all wounds and restores us to value — the love that enriches and ennobles our impoverished and disfigured encounters and memories of refusals to love, which are tragically grounded in our refusal to be loved by so great a Love. One basic and universal thing we can say about love in light of the claim "u got 2 love" is that love is essential [of the most importance, basic, indispensable, necessary, somethin without which an entire system or complex whole would collapse]. JPII, in his first encyclical *The Redeemer of Man,* #10, flat out made the bold claim, "Man cannot live without love. He remains a being that is incomprehensible for himself, his life is senseless, if love is not revealed to him, if he does not encounter love, if he does not experience it and make it his own, if he does not participate intimately in it." The essential nature of love is broken down even more intensely when in his book *Love and Responsibility* (p. 17) he talks about "the problem of introducing love into love." This reminds me of St. Francis, who, like a wild man drunk and crazy with love, ran door to door through the streets of Assisi with the intensity and urgency of love cryin out: "Love is not loved."

The human person is called into existence through love for love.

God created man in His own image and likeness: calling him to existence through love, He called him at the same time for love. God is love and in Himself He lives a mystery of personal loving communion. Creating the human race in His own image and continually keeping it in being, God inscribed in the humanity of man and woman the vocation, and thus the capacity and responsibility, of love and communion.

— JPII, *Familiaris Consortio* #11

So everything pouring out of my heart onto these pages is intended to inform and assist you the reader, along with me the writer, in allowin this fundamental and innate vocation to love to shine with greater brilliance — with the radiance of Love — the love that carries us along and goes to the end, the love that empowers us to be carriers of one another. This amazin gift and task of love's burden-carryin energies is not burdensome as many people sometimes fearfully feel and think. Quite to the dramatic contrary, this burden-carryin power of love is bountiful and beautiful, unleashin transformative powers in the thick and thin of our days and nights that makes everythin ugly beautiful.

The Bible says, "God is love" (1 Jn 4:8); people in my South Bronx NYC neighborhood say, "God don't like ugly." The truth of this statement is based on the absolute truth and Reality that God is love. In fact, B16 reminds us that the realization of the reality and practice of the love that carries us along is not a burden, but rather a tremendous blessin that lifts us up and carries us along: "It is not a burden to be carried by a great love and realization, but it is like having wings" (August 16, 2005, Vatican Radio Interview).

Love energizes and empowers us to rebuild what has been and is bein destroyed within and around us. It's an enlivenin energy and enthusiasm to "beautify" — to make all that has been made ugly more beautiful than it was in the first place. Too many people are tragically consumed by that which they consume and left disappointed and betrayed as one of the unfortunate results of impoverished love. The value of life has been cheapened, and the undetected and unacknowledged bondage of shame is tragically strengthened. Christopher Dawson insightfully reveals, "As civilization becomes materially richer and more powerful it becomes spiritually or religiously weaker and poorer" (*Civilization in Crisis*). It's kinda like sayin — sad but true — the more stuff we get, the more impoverished our ability to love becomes. At the end of the day, we want to choose love because of what JPII refers to as "the beautifying immunity from shame as the result of love."

Carried by Love

Yet, with all this love drama goin on, to be carried by love and to love with the power to carry others — this amazin capacity for human love to fly and progress is not done in an "emotional only way." Rather, it is hopefully done with the emotion that sets and keeps in motion the flow of the power that has been instilled within us to participate in the Love with which God himself loves us. This first step into this first Love by which we were created in turn prepares the human heart for the expansion necessary for the purification and elevation of *eros*. This step renders us ready for the truth of love, which sets us free for true love, which renders us ready for renunciation.

The tragic separation of truth from love is what strengthens all of the deceitful tactics of false love which impoverishes human love, infectin it with its easy and selfish compromises, thrivin on possessin the person or object loved rather than makin a gift of self. An understandin and livin of true love, the love that makes sacrifice doable and desirable, develops into deeper communion with the perfect love that casts out all fear and makes this increase of sacrificial love and the free gift of self not just doable and desirable, but makes sacrificial love become amazingly a source of joy.

God's *eros* is the supreme expression of his *agape*.

One could rightly say that the revelation of God's eros toward man is, in reality, the supreme expression of His agape. In all truth, only the love that unites the free gift of oneself with the impassioned desire for reciprocity instills a joy, which eases the heaviest of burdens. Jesus said: "When I am lifted up from the earth, I will draw all men to myself" (Jn 12:32). The response the Lord ardently desires from us is above all that we welcome His love and allow ourselves to be drawn to Him. Accepting His love, however, is not enough. We need to respond to such love and devote ourselves to communicating it to others. Christ "draws me to Himself" in order to unite Himself to me, so that I learn to love the brothers with His own love.

— B16, Lent 2007

JPII + B16

Some of you may know that B16's wonderful first encyclical *Deus Caritas Est* (DCE) was initially started by JPII prior to his death. Robert Moynihan, in a February 2006 *Inside the Vatican* article, revealed, "Just before his death, Pope John

Paul II had been working on an encyclical about Christian love. Benedict XVI decided to complete the project." In a general audience on January 16, 2006, B16 made clear his intention with DCE: "In this encyclical, I want to explain the concept of love in its various dimensions." The Pope said his goal was to demonstrate that "love is one movement with different dimensions."

It is love alone that can satisfy the different dimensions and every dimension of the human heart. Every human person, with all the many different and complex needs, situations, and circumstances encountered every day on the worldwide level is in need of love — we all need to be loved and to love in return. We all got 2 love. Yet, the word love itself generates a complex maze of confusin meanings. As B16 eloquently put it on January 23, 2006, in an address to a Vatican-sponsored conference on charity, "Today the word 'love' is so wasted, consumed and abused that one is almost afraid to let it form on the lips." Yet, at the same time, love must be talked about in a way that helps us to live it. Love must be talked about in order to inform, challenge, and purify ideas about love so that, as B16 said, "It can enlighten our lives," so that we can live it and love livin it. And the "it" is not really an "it," when love for others no longer seeks itself but rather "becomes concern for the other, a willingness to sacrifice" for the other with love and because of love. Self-givin and seekin the good of the other — givin the better and strivin for the best — this is the key. However, if we are in communion with B16 and his great predecessor JPII, and the reckless consistent outpourin of love JPII lived throughout his entire life, especially durin his great pontificate, roarin like a lion from beginnin to end, cryin out "Do not be afraid," then Love will have its way with us. The fact that we "got 2 love" will grip us, unleashin the authentic freedom for which we were set free — free by truth to be in the truth, with love and responsibility for the truth, to love with true love.

I am aware of the many responses and reactions that can flow from the provocative claim "u got 2 love." Who am I to say that to you and who is anybody to say that to anybody? There are so many, some times too many questions, feelins, opinions, and loads of other dynamics. In addition to all this, I wanna say that from this ever-flowin stream of possible responses and reactions, the most amazin response is contained in what God has revealed through the prophet Zephaniah combined with the great JPII. The "u got 2" dimension of all this is made accessible by the fact that Love is so kind, and knows us so well, that renewal is built right into the equation. The prophet Zephaniah reveals in 3:14-18 that the Lord our God (Love) will "renew you in his love." Check out the amazin result the impact of us bein renewed by God's love has on God: "he will sing joyfully because of you." So to get this right we have to imagine and create a picture in our mind's eye of God singin, and God singin because of me, because of you, because of us bein renewed in his love. Can we imagine this? Sometimes I have a hard time tryin, yet I can sense deep in my bones that it's true. This becomes even more challengin if we dare to come to terms with the revealed reason for God singin — you and me renewed in his love; you and me renewed in the passionate pursuit of love every day! When we allow ourselves to be renewed in love by Love, God wants to sing. So, in other words, love makes Love sing! The ultimate expression of this song is sung in the Song of Songs 8:6, "Love is strong as death."

This bein renewed in love is itself the work of Love. It's both love workin on us and within us, workin with the energy of Love for healin which releases more love, which brings about greater healin for an even greater outpourin of Love! Are you ready for this? All of this love stuff is not about just healin me and my wounds, and you and your wounds, even though Love does that. At the same time, it's also about a greater healin of the greater wounds that are infectin, crushin, and destroyin the hearts and lives of so many people all over the world, as well as the fallen dimensions of their cultures with the multiple destructive dimensions that are impoverishin love.

This tragic impoverishment of love is not runnin its destructive heart-crushin course just in Western, capital-driven, money-lovin, North American consumer cultures. It's also crushin hearts in the South, crushin hearts in the East, as well as crushin hearts in the West. This crushin of the human heart is dramatically effectin all cultures on every continent. Yes, this is huge. Hopefully you now have a better sense of why I'm sayin "u got 2 love." There's an urgency here, and most of us most of the time ain't feelin it for "good reasons" that are never good enough. "It ain't that bad," we cry, tryin to convince ourselves we can manage on our own. After all, the electricity still goes on, the refrigerator and TV work, we got our "stuff," and life still seems "normal." What the heck are we talkin about when we talk about "normal"?

What might help us here is to find a way — or better still to make a way — to acknowledge that love is impoverished by us when we are overwhelmed by fear. In 1 John 4:18 we read, "There is no fear in love, but perfect love casts out fear." When we are not connected to — in communion with — this fear-castin-out power of perfect love that "never fails" and that goes "to the end," we are more or less gonna be controlled by fear, which is like bein in prison.

Modern culture is born to exalt man and his dignity.

More than ever, today's world has a need to rediscover the meaning of life and death in the perspective of eternal life....

Outside of love, modern culture, born to exalt man and his dignity, is paradoxically transformed into a culture of death, because without the horizon of God, he finds himself a prisoner in the world, overwhelmed by fear, and unfortunately, gives way to multiple personal and collective pathologies.

— Pope John Paul II, March 11, 2002, Angelus Message

At the funeral of one of my mentors and heroes, Fr. Hans Urs von Balthasar, (from now on, referred to respectfully, with love and affection, as von B), a great Swiss Catholic theologian — very dear to the great JPII — our current Holy Father B16 (then Cardinal Ratzinger) preached and quoted from one of his mentors and heroes, St. Augustine: "Our entire task in this life, dear brothers, consists in the healing of the eyes of the heart so that they may be able to see God." To see God is to see Love, because God is Love; and to see Love is boiled down as our entire task in this life. It all boils down to seein Love lovin us, and seein and knowin ourselves as loved with a Love which empowers us to love with the very Love with which we have been loved. So the "u got 2 love" thing is really somethin deep inside of each of us, and the impoverishin of this deepest reality of the human person is one of the core sources for so much disappointment and unhappiness, the core source of the lack of love in our lives and our world. This impoverishin of love contributes to the increase of wickedness and evil which causes love to grow cold. That's why Jesus said, "Because wickedness is multiplied, most men's love will grow cold" (Mt 24:12).

Love and Options

Our hearts are targeted and crushed by the ever-increasin, unimaginable, incalculable amount of options that confront us daily. Options, on the one hand, are good and a gift from

God — they are expressions of His Love. God, the source of all life-givin options, presents the greatest options through the mysterious designs of Divine Providence, which are historical, real-deal manifestations of His Love. Options release the potential we have to create new ways of being in the world, occasions and opportunities to change for the better, to be and do more love. In light of Jesus referrin to Himself as "the way" in John 14:6, we can become "way makers" and dignify the capacity we have for options.

To be a "way maker" is to be in tune with the sentiments of the heart of God who is love. It's kinda like St. John of the Cross sayin, "Where there is no love, put love, and you will find love." This way, makin energy generated by options connected with Jesus as the truth and the life releases the energy necessary for us to exalt Jesus as the Absolute source of options for greater love with the very same Love with which He Loves us. This is huge, and we have the capacity for such love because we were created in the image of this Love and have been redeemed by this Love for more love! These options for freedom and love in truth for true love will nourish the capacity within us to live this love — the true love we desperately need, the true love we deeply long for, the true love that is daily provided for us and which is waitin to be loved. Awareness of bein loved by true love is so important for our commitment to contributin to the buildin of the new civilization of love.

ℬein in tune with the heart of Jesus helps us build the civilization of love.

You are burning with desire to be loved, and those in tune with the sentiments of your heart learn how to build the new civilization of love.

— JPII to Jesus, April 22, 2001 (Divine Mercy Sunday)

However, on the other hand, the encounter with all the cultural options we have at the beginnin of the post-modern era for seein, lookin, shoppin, buyin, and possessin dramatically imposes limits on our God-given capacity to love and casts us into deeper disorder. The human capacity for love I'm talkin about is love with a freedom and fullness that goes beyond mere human strength and reasonable sensibilities. For example, I'm talkin about Jesus' love doctrine of lovin one's enemies. More precisely, these bewilderin cultural encounters with seemin limitless options tragically contributes and nourishes the impoverishin energies and dimensions of our fallen nature, most especially with regard to the undiscovered dimensions of love. Healin the wounds from these reductive and destructive effects of impoverished love is important work for all of us. Pope Paul VI touched upon this point of our role as what we could call "love doctors" for healin and buildin up the civilization of love when he said, "We are called to be physicians of that civilization about which we dream, the civilization of love" (December 31, 1975).

A lust for seein casts us into disorder.

There is a lust for seeing that perverts the original meaning of sight and casts a person into disorder.

— Joseph Pieper

When people are overwhelmed by life and the heart-crushin energies of the culture of death, one of the most desperate and unfortunate options is hatred. Hatred is a very strong word and emotion. Most of the time, when the human capacity to love with true love is not accessed, when it's left dormant and untapped, self-hatred is the result. As AJH powerfully revealed, "The treasuries of the soul are consumed in the fires of self-hatred." These tragic fires of self-hatred burn and consume both the person hatin him or herself as well as the people who become the victims of their hatred. With hatred nobody wins — everybody loses.

---

l ove by its very nature excludes hatred and ill will.

God, who already as Creator has linked Himself to His creature with a particular love. Love, by its very nature, excludes hatred and ill will towards the one to whom He once gave the gift of Himself: Nihil odisti eorum quae fecisti, *"you hold nothing of what you have made in abhorrence." These words indicate the profound basis of the relationship between justice and mercy in God, in His relations with man and the world. They tell us that we must seek the life-giving roots and intimate reasons for this relationship by going back to "the beginning," in the very mystery of creation. They foreshadow in the context of the Old Covenant the full revelation of God, who is "love."*

— JPII, *Rich in Mercy* #4

In a Vatican-sponsored event on charity held on January 23, 2006, B16 revealed the kind of love we need in order to offset the destructive energies raging from hatred: "In an age when hatred and greed have become superpowers, in an age when we see religion abused to the point of becoming the deification of hatred, neutral rationalization alone cannot protect us. We need the living God who loved us to the point of death." Love to the point of death on part of the livin God is the revelatory revolution we need for the radical communion of love between humans to become real and help us transcend ourselves. It is absolutely necessary for us to go out of and beyond ourselves so that the understandin, patience, and kindness of love can accomplish its amazin work in us and in our world, makin it a better place. As we read in 1 John 4:8 "Whoever does not love does not know God, because God is love." As JPII said, "The most important thing about love is the sincere gift of self. In this sense the person is realized through love" (*Crossing the Threshold of Hope*, p. 325).

When God is not acknowledged as God, man is betrayed.

Unfortunately, God's marvelous plan was marred by the appearance of sin in history. Through sin, man rebels against his Creator and ends up worshipping creatures: "They exchanged the truth about God for a lie and worshipped and served the creature rather than the Creator" (Rom 1:25). As a result man not only deforms the image of God in his own person, but is tempted to offenses against it in others as well, replacing relationships of communion by attitudes of distrust, indifference, hostility, and even murderous hatred. When God is not acknowledged as God, the profound meaning of man is betrayed, and communion between people is compromised.

— JPII, *Evangelium Vitae* #32

Communion of Love

The love that persons encounter in God opens the eye of the soul to see love at work. So when we are loved — rooted and grounded in love — and love in return, the stirrin of love's revealin movement unleashes the human capacity to see those we love in all we look at. This communion of love also provides light for us to see people we don't like in a different light, which is necessary to reduce and eliminate feelings and actions of hatred. This communion of love mysteriously and really establishes peace in the human heart that is beyond all understandin. Yet, at the same time, this communion of love stands under and moves within the details of every encounter, all of the essential and ultimate challenges and problems of life.

The peace and security provided and sustained by this communion of love releases the capacity for persons to freely suffer separation from the one loved with a sufferin that swells with a mystifyin sweetness. The heart is longin for more love as well as the person loved, without possessin the person loved but yearnin to provide yet even more love. This love that does not possess can love and be at rest while lettin go of the person, event, or object loved for the sake of love. In other words, we learn to suffer. This trustin surrender and lettin go, releases the capacity of the human person for more love — for Divine Love, the love which bears fruit that lasts unto eternal life, the love that goes to the end, the love that never fails. As a result there is a greater abidin in and closeness with the one loved. In this love, feelings of conflict and even hatred can transcend mere tolerance and give birth to new beginnings and encounters that are rooted in more than what we can do for ourselves. We're not used to this kinda stuff, but that does not mean that this ain't real. It's the losin oneself to find oneself that Jesus talks about in Matthew 10:39, "He who finds his life will lose it, and he who loses his life for my sake will find it."

This communion of love expresses a dimension of the beauty of love that is a power instilled within us, furnishin us to go out of and beyond ourselves. The makin real of this power of love buried within us depends on the depth of our experience and awareness of bein loved. When we are open and receptive to Love lovin us, the truth of this encounter constructs the arena of freedom for which Christ has set us free. This arena is where all the failures of fallen and impoverished love on our part and the part of others — includin hatred whether it's self-hatred, hatin others, or bein hated by others — can be, and needs to be, enriched by the Love that "never fails." The deepest longin burning in the heart of the world is waitin, cryin, and starvin for love. It is my hope, my intention, and my prayer that this book will be a help for us all along the way, so that love can become more and more the dominant force in our lives. I hope that in some way it will help in renderin us so loved by this Love that we will become tireless in sustainin the efforts that transcend merely human abilities in perusin and followin the Love that goes "to the end," and by virtue of this love faithfully go to the end. Amen.

33 Considerations to Help Us Learn Something About Love

Even though love is something that can't be taught, JPII teaches us that it's absolutely valuable that we learn somethin about it. The followin 33 considerations are intended to do just that — to help us learn somethin about love. Albert Einstein once wrote in a letter, "I must love someone; otherwise it is a miserable existence." This is true because we are wired by Love to love. B16 pressed this point even further when he met with a group of disadvantaged young people in Sydney during World Youth Day 2008, reminding us that the whole revelation and program of love "is hard-wired into every human person." We've got enough people — or rather more precisely, way too many people — who feel that their life is a miserable existence because they do not love. What can we do about that? While it is true that "we got 2 love," it's also true that love is so impoverished that I sometimes wonder if love is even possible.

1. Is Love Possible?

The fact that love is possible flows from the power of the absolute goodness of Love. The *Catechism of the Catholic Church* (CCC) helps us to see this in paragraph 412: "There is nothing to prevent human nature's being raised up to something greater, even after sin; God permits evil in order to draw forth some greater good" (St. Thomas Aquinas, *STh* III, 1, 3, *ad* 3; cf. *Rom* 5:20). The possibility of love is proven in our ability to bounce back. I like to call it "bounce-back power." It's this "greater good" that's drawn forth from evil; it's the "something greater" in spite of everythin that happens. It's the power of this greater good that attracts me, that fascinates me, that releases through me the reality of the possibility of love — the love that's "stronger than death" (cf. Song of Songs 8:6). I've seen this so many times in so many people, rich, poor, sick, healthy, young, and old. And I've never seen it as clear as I'm seein it right now, as I'm writin this section, in both my parents, who were diagnosed with cancer in the same week. The generosity of the gift and givin of themselves I've seen all throughout my life — but never so clearly and forcefully as I'm seein the givin of themselves right now. Love is possible — and beautifully so.

Learnin to love by knowin oneself as loved.

How can one learn to love and give oneself generously? Nothing is so conducive to loving, said St. Thomas, as knowing oneself to be loved.

— JPII, November 27, 2003

Love is possible because it's the most basic and fundamental human need. We can't live without love. I'm talkin specifically about the need we have to receive love and to give love. Our life is dramatically and radically incomplete without love. What water, air, and food are to the human body, love is to the human person. Any and every life without this sense of bein loved and without the prospect of the possibility of lovin is an impoverished life. St. Augustine understands the human person essentially as a being who must love: in other words, u got 2 love! Erasmo Leiva-Merikakis in his fine book *Love's Sacred Orders* makes a great comment on a great line from Augustine. Augustine said, "I did not yet love, but I was in love with the idea of loving." Erasmo derives from this Augustine's essential definition of the human person "as the being who must love in order fully to be himself" (p. 26). According to B16, in DCE #31, we must "dedicate ourselves to others with heartfelt concern, enabling them to experience the richness of their humanity." It's the formation and re-formation of the human heart that can enrich the experience of love. This formation of the heart "leads to that encounter with God in Christ which awakens our love and opens our spirits to others." The awakenin and enrichin of humanity is possible — love is possible. If love was not possible we would have no hope and could not live. We cannot live without love.

Man cannot live without love.

Man cannot live without Love. He remains a being that is incomprehensible for himself, his life is senseless, if love is not revealed to him, if he does not encounter love, if he does not experience it and make it his own, if he does not participate intimately in it.

— JPII, *Redemptor Hominis* #10

Sometimes when life becomes too much, it's understandable how people can doubt if love is possible. I certainly appreciate how and why people sometimes feel and think this way. To say it's difficult to love is one of the greatest understatements in the history of understatements. Sometimes it seems that it's impossible to love. Quite frankly, that's because sometimes it is.

There are those who doubt that love is possible.

Everybody feels the longing to love and to be loved. Yet, how difficult it is to love, and how many mistakes and failures have to be reckoned with in love! There are those who even come to doubt that love is possible. But if emotional delusions or lack of affection can cause us to think that love is utopian, an impossible dream, should we then become resigned? No! Love is possible, and the purpose of my message is to help reawaken in each one of you — you who are the future and hope of humanity — trust in a love that is true, faithful, and strong; a love that generates peace and joy; a love that binds people together and allows them to feel free in respect for one another.

— B16, 22nd World Youth Day, 2007

Yet why let that stop us? Every good reason and the best of good reasons is never really good enough. Not even those reasons that see love as a delusional utopia, that view love as somethin that can't work, won't work, and doesn't work. In spite of all this, there's hope. As B16 said in *Spe Salvi*, our "great, true hope which holds firm in spite of all disappointments can only be God — God who has loved us and who continues to love us 'to the end,' until all 'is accomplished' (cf. Jn 13:1 and 19:30). Whoever is moved by love begins to perceive what 'life' really is." Bein moved by love makes hope in the possibility of love a reality even to the point of our whole being bein reordered by love — so powerful is the attraction of love.

The attraction of Love can reorder our whole being.

The attraction of love can capture and purify the will of man and subordinate it to the great purpose of God ... to have the thrust of our whole being reordered by God (reordered by Love).

— Evelyn Underhill, *An Anthology of Love*, p. 30

As B16 said in DCE #39:

Love ... transforms our impatience and doubts into the sure hope that God holds the world in his hands.... Love is possible, and we are able to practice it because we are created in the image and likeness of God.... Love is the light — and in the end, the only light that can always illuminate a world grown dim and give us the courage needed to keep living and working.

2. Do You Love?

The only question that makes life worth livin.

"Do you love?" It is only thanks to this question that life is worth living.... "Do you love?" has a universal significance, an abiding value. It constructs in the history of mankind the world of God. Only love constructs this world. It constructs it with difficulty. It must struggle to give it shape. It must struggle against the forces of evil, sin, hatred, against the lust of the eyes, and against the pride of life (1 Jn 2:16).... Christ is the cornerstone of this construction. He is the cornerstone of this shape that the world, our human world, can take thanks to love.... It is from him that, in spite of the darkness and the clouds that continue to gather on the horizon of history. And you know how threatening they are today in our age! It is from him that the abiding construction will spring up, it is on him that it will take the shape of eternity in the earthly and short lived dimensions of the history of man on earth."

— JPII, Paris, May 30, 1980

JPII in his first encyclical, *Redemptor Hominis,* proclaims flat out that, "Man cannot live without love." If we believe in this ultimate proclamation, then we got to ask the ultimate question: "Do you love?" Who do I love? What do I love? How do I love? There are all kinds of stuff and events that people say they love. But as Msgr. Lorenzo Albacete points out, the desires of our heart are reduced to what is culturally possible; and as cultural possibilities with regard to love reduce the desires of our hearts, the question "Do you love?" will be reduced to mean "Do you get what you want?" This reduction is the result of pride, the great impoverisher of love. Pride, according to Tanquerey, is "an inordinate love of self, which causes us to consider ourselves, explicitly or implicitly, as our first beginning and our last end." All this raises another question, and the answer will involve struggle — struggle against sin and the forces of evil, hatred, lust, pride and all the vices. Answerin this question will unleash the great on-goin work of buildin the world of God in the history of man. To do so we will be required to practice what B16 refers to as the humility of renunciation.

A skin questions — one of humanity's noblest tasks.

Men and women have at their disposal an array of resources for generating greater knowledge of truth so that their lives may be ever more human. Among these is philosophy, which is directly concerned with asking the question of life's meaning and sketching an answer to it. Philosophy emerges, then, as one of noblest of human tasks. According to its Greek etymology, the term philosophy means "love of wisdom." Born and nurtured when the human being first asked questions about the reason for things and their purpose, philosophy shows in different modes and forms that the desire for truth is part of human nature itself. It is an innate property of human reason to ask why things are as they are, even though the answers which gradually emerge are set within a horizon which reveals how the different human cultures are complementary.

— JPII, *Faith and Reason* #3

Questions are good, good questions are important, and there is no better or more important question we can ask ourselves than "Do you love?" At the end of our lives we will be judged on how we have loved. So gettin used to askin ourselves this question as we move through life is a good idea. Remember, love is the fundamental vocation of every human person on the planet. JPII loved askin questions. That's one of the reasons why he loved philosophy, which is a love of wisdom. Askin questions about the meanin of life and love and seekin answers is one of humanity's noblest tasks. From this point of view, then, the noblest question is "Do you love?" May the perfection of love cast out all traces of fear in our hearts so we can ask ourselves this question every day resultin with us really learnin somethin about love.

JPII went to Cuba in 1998 and met with young people as was his preferred pleasure and custom. The love contained in his big heart poured out to believers and nonbelievers alike. He met them on the common ground of love. His Christian and cultural humanism went straight to their hearts challengin them while lovin them in the midst of their pain, poverty, and lack of opportunity, tellin them the whole truth and nothin but the truth. He told them that feelin themselves loved by Jesus will in turn enable them to love. He's talkin to them (and to us too) from his own experience:

> *Dear young people, whether you are believers or not, accept the call to be virtuous. This means being strong within, having a big heart, being rich in the highest sentiments, bold in the truth, courageous in freedom, constant in responsibility, generous in love, invincible in hope. Happiness is achieved through sacrifice. Do not look outside for what is to be found inside. Do not expect from others what you yourselves can and are called to be or to do. Do not leave for tomorrow the building of a new society in which the noblest dreams are not frustrated and in which you can be the principal agents of your own history.... "The love of God made known in Christ Jesus" (Rom. 8:39). This love alone can light up the night of human loneliness.... In one form or another all human beings experience pain and suffering in their lives and this cannot but lead them to pose a question. Pain is a*

mystery, often inscrutable to reason. It forms part of the mystery of the human person, which alone comes clear in Jesus Christ who reveals to man man's true identity. Christ alone enables us to know the meaning of all that is human.... A life fully human and committed to Christ requires this generosity and dedication.... I encourage you to experience Christ's love, to be conscious of what he has done for you, for all humanity, for the men and women of every age. Feeling yourselves loved by him, you will in turn truly be able to love.... Unfortunately, it is easier for people to fall into moral relativism and the identity crisis which affects so many young people, victims of cultural models which are empty of meaning or of an ideology which does not offer high and clear moral guidelines. Such moral relativism gives rise to selfishness, division, marginalization, discrimination, fear and distrust of others. Consequently, the emptiness brought on by this behavior explains many of the evils which beset young people: alcohol, the abuse of sex, drug use ... the lack of a serious life project.

3. Dare to Love

Love is the only force capable of changin the human heart — dare to love.

I want to invite you to "dare to love" ... in imitation of the One who vanquished hatred and death forever through love (cf. Rev 5:13). Love is the only force capable of changing the heart of the human person and of all humanity, by making fruitful the relations between men and women, between rich and poor, between cultures and civilizations. This is shown to us in the lives of the saints. They are true friends of God who channel and reflect this very first love. Try to know them better, entrust yourselves to their intercession, and strive to live as they did.... Each one of us, my dear friends, has been given the possibility of reaching this same level of love, but only by having recourse to the indispensable support of divine Grace.

— B16, April 1, 2007, 22nd World Youth Day

Our magnificent successor of JPII is rollin with the same steam as his great predecessor. B16 is flowin with the same torrential love as JPII with regard to challengin young people and all people to love. In his 22nd World Youth Day message, B16 flat out dared the young people of the world to love. The call to dare to love is a darin call indeed; it requires courage for us to be bold in clingin to Jesus' admonition taken up by JPII: "Do not be afraid." The love we're talkin about and are bein called to dare to do is double-sided and double stacked; it's the two-edged sword of love and responsibility — the truth and life synthesis as revealed in the Gospel of Jesus Christ and the whole of divine revelation. As the great JPII taught and showed us, this love and life — truth and responsibility synthesis of the Gospel demands somethin from us that's beyond our ability.

What Love demands is beyond our abilities.

*Love and life according to the Gospel cannot be thought of first and foremost as a kind of precept, because **what they demand is beyond man's abilities**. They are possible only as the result of a gift of God who heals, restores and transforms the human heart by his grace.*

— JPII, *Veritatis Splendor* #23

I can hear it now because I feel this way sometime too: "That's not fair." It's not about bein fair. Rather it's all about how far we're willin to go with the gift of love that heals and strengthens our narrow and weak hearts to participate in the ever expandin and limitless reality and possibilities of Love in light of and in spite of our failures in lovin. Yes, the possibility of comin to love this level of love that presses us beyond our ability is possible because it's given as a gift. The good news here that gives hope is that the ultimate teacher of Love is God himself. The patient presence of so great a teacher who never fails and whose never-endin action enables us to pursue that which is beyond our natural abilities. His perfect never-endin action on our impoverished imperfect hearts and lives never ends. And as my girl Evelyn Underhill reminds us and challenges us, "We are not working on something finished and done with; we look so far as we dare, at an eternal process — the increasing action of divine Love."

The increasin action of Divine Love.

...the patient loving presence of God, the Perfect, who by his ceaseless action on the imperfect, alone gives form and brings forth life. We are not working on something finished and done with; we look so far as we dare, at an eternal process — the increasing action of the divine Love.

— Evelyn Underhill, *Anthology of Love*, p. 45

4. Lessons of Love

The great JPII told us that we "enter the world as the subject of truth and love" (Wednesday, February 20, 1980). As people who are the subject of truth and love, the lessons of love we are called to work on in all truth, are lessons that are never finished and done with. The Child of Bethlehem — Love itself — entered the world to teach us love and to teach us how to love; the awesomeness of a little child helps us overcome the fear of the greatness of these lessons. Of all that has been given and of all that is required, love is the greatest. The first lesson is "Be not afraid." Be not afraid of the greatness of the task as well as be not afraid of the greatness we are called to achieve with regard to love because love is our fundamental vocation. To live the teachins of JPII and B16 on love is not easy, especially as we try to make them a reality, with the help of the Holy Spirit and the prayers of Mother Mary and the saints, to make them a reality in the history of our lives and the lives of people who suffer. Archbishop Oscar Romero is a great help here:

> To follow faithfully the pope's magisterium in theory is very easy. But when you try to live those saving teachings, try to incarnate them, try to make them reality in the history of a suffering people like ours — that is when conflicts arise. Dear friends, if we are really Catholics, followers of an authentic gospel — and therefore a difficult gospel — if we really want to live up to the name of followers of Christ, let us not be afraid to transform into flesh and blood, into living history, this teaching, which from the pages of the gospel becomes present reality in the teaching of the councils and of the popes, who try to live like true shepherds through the vicissitudes of their times (Archbishop Oscar Romero, July 2, 1978).

The first lessons of love are awakened through the lovin exchange of a mother and child. "After a mother has smiled at her child for many days and weeks, she finally receives her child's smile in response. She has awakened love in the heart of her child" (von B, *Love Alone*, p. 76). This is beautiful, yet I'm seein and feelin those hearts in which this all important lesson of love has not yet been awakened. It's never too late. Yet, the selfishness that postpones this all-important lesson of love will not be acknowledged and dealt with until we look Crucified Love in the eye. Love awakens love. As von B says, "It is only when we look the crucified One in the eye that we recognize the abyss of selfishness — even of that which we are accustomed to call love" (*Love Alone*, p. 66).

When we say with JPII that love is somethin that can't be taught, we basically mean that there's never a moment when we "get it," when we've learned the lessons of love and it's over and done with. It means precisely and essentially that we learn somethin about love, and the "somethin" we learn about love is that it never ends; there's never enough, there's always more. Love has no beginnin and no end. And that's why the beginnin of learnin somethin about somethin that can't be taught, in the sense that it will never be a static done deal, means the adventure of learnin somethin about love in this life carries us up and down every mountain, leadin us endlessly into loves fulfillment — the supreme moment of happiness. "Love is never finished and complete; throughout life, it changes and matures, and thus remains faithful to itself" (B16, DCE #17).

From Bethlehem a stream of light, love and truth spreads through the centuries.

In the stable of Bethlehem there appeared the great light which the world awaits. In that Child lying in the stable, God

has shown his glory — the glory of love, which gives itself
away, stripping itself of all grandeur in order to guide us
along the way of love. The light of Bethlehem has never been
extinguished. In every age it has touched men and women, "it
has shone around them." Wherever people put their faith in
that Child, charity also sprang up — charity towards others,
loving concern for the weak and the suffering, the grace of
forgiveness. From Bethlehem a stream of light, love and truth
spreads through the centuries. If we look to the Saints — from
Paul and Augustine to Francis and Dominic, from Francis
Xavier and Teresa of Avila to Mother Teresa of Calcutta —
we see this flood of goodness, this path of light kindled ever
anew by the mystery of Bethlehem, by that God who became
a Child. In that Child, God countered the violence of this world
with his own goodness. He calls us to follow that Child.

— B16, December 24, 2005

One of the best ways to work at learnin the lessons of love is to look at love in action in the lives of the saints. When I say saints I'm talkin about big saints and little saints, known and unknown, canonized and noncanonized . JPII referred to them as "people of every age, Nation, and social condition. Moreover, it is not only those who are 'canonized' who are 'Saints,' but all believers who live and die faithful to the Divine Will" (November 1, 1992). To live and die faithful in doin God's Will is the end of all lessons of love. It's the daily details of knowin and doin that Will with love that's the key. Conversion and ongoin conversion plays a major role in learnin the lessons of love. Von B tells us that conversion is a relearnin of "what love after all really is" (*Love Alone*, p. 61). The beauty of this love-lesson is a love-story: "The love-story between God and man consists in the very fact that this communion of thought and sentiment, and thus our will and God's will increasingly coincide: God's will is no longer for me an alien will, something imposed on me from without by the commandments, but it is now my own will" (B16, DCE #17).

Vincent van Gogh is one of my tragic heroes. In the midst of his brokenness and pain he teaches us about love and helps us learn how to find a way to enrich our impoverished love. Vinnie helps us learn somethin about love from the very depths of the darkness of impoverished love that had quite a grip on him. From one of his many amazin letters to his brother Theo he writes, "Life is even more a matter of rowing against the current.... Even though things go differently from the expected, it is necessary to take heart again and new courage. For the great things are not done by impulse, but by a series of small things brought together, and great things are not something accidental but must certainly be willed" (Irving Stone, *Dear Theo*, A Plume Book, 1995, p. 163). Seekin to know and do God's will strengthens our weak wills to strive always to choose love. When we fail in makin that choice, it is love that revives us with the lift to bounce back.

One of the main reasons I'm includin the "Love Zone — An Anthology of Love," is specifically to help us every day be ready for more love, to learn a little somethin more about love. The many different quotations on love provide valuable lessons for us to learn and relearn. U got 2 believe, u got 2 pray, and u got 2 love, and to help all three of these u-got-2's, u got 2 read. Readin is feedin the heart, mind, and soul which affects the body. We are body-soul creatures, and given the fact that we are also cultural creatures necessitates the development of good feedin/readin habits.

The crisis in education we're experiencing as a result of moral and cultural relativism is ultimately a crisis in learnin the lessons of love. The ultimate education manifests lessons that shape life accordin to God's plan of love. "Man's ability to see is in decline."

Education is to shape life accordin to the plan of Love.

Education, Christian education particularly, is to shape life according to the plan of God who is love (cf. I Jn 4:8, 16) needs that closeness which is proper to love....The family has a proper and fundamental mission and a primary responsibility. Through its parents in fact the child who is starting life has the first and decisive experience of love, of a love which is in reality not only human, it is a reflection of God's love for every human person.

— B16, June 11, 2007

"Those who nowadays concern themselves with culture and education will experience this fact again and again" (Josef Pieper, *Only the Lover Sings*, Ignatius Press, 1990, p. 31). This decline in seein impoverishes the person and therefore impoverishes love. The openin of the eyes — the work of a lifetime — enriches love and lifts up the person and makes a positive cultural effect. St. Francis helps us learn somethin about love in that he spent all his energies attemptin to respond to the generosity of God, to the generosity of Love. At the end of a lifetime of squanderin himself in response to the lavishness of Love, Francesco lay naked on the naked earth in imitation of the naked Crucified Christ sayin to his brothers, "Brothers let us begin to serve the Lord our God, for up to now we have made little or no progress."

The great teachers of love help us to learn that with Love there is always more, there is never enough. This is so because they are not attached to their own resources and are completely captivated by the never-endin, ever-fruitful, indefatigable self-givin energies of love. Without him ever knowin it, St. Francis helped Lenin learn somethin about love. At the end of a life of hateful destruction, it sounds like Lenin almost repented. In order to reverse all the hate, destruction, and death he caused, he wanted ten St. Francises.

Lenin and Ten Francis of Assisi's.

*I have deluded myself. Without doubt, it was necessary to free the oppressed masses. However, our methods resulted in other oppressions and gruesome massacres. You know I am deadly ill; I feel lost in a ocean of blood formed by countless victims. This was necessary to save our Russia, but it is too late to turn back. **We would need ten Francis of Assisi's.***

— Lenin, at the end of his life in 1924

---

5. Language of Love

The body is no longer the language of love.

Within this same cultural climate, the body is no longer perceived as a properly personal reality, a sign and place of relations with others, with God, and with the world. It is reduced to pure materiality: it is simply a complex of organs, functions and energies to be used according to the sole criteria of pleasure and efficiency. Consequently, sexuality too is depersonalized and exploited: from being the sign, place and language of love, that is, of the gift of self and acceptance of another, in all the other's richness as a person, it increasingly becomes the occasion and instrument for self-assertion and the selfish satisfaction of personal desires and instincts.

— JPII, *Evangelium Vitae* #23

The language of love involves the fullness of the grandeur and dignity of the human person — body and soul. In a culture that promotes a destructive, permissive, and perverted glorification of the body at the expense of the soul, discoverin, recoverin, and renewin the language of love becomes ever more difficult and all the more necessary. The es calatin self-hatred with the reduction of the person through the crushin of the heart generates a "I hate my body" attitude in the midst of a deceptive and false glorification of the body. The result is that a demonically distorted cultural psychology and philosophy of the body excites people with a hope of bein fulfilled and happy and ends up leavin them deeply disappointed and defeated. I use the word demonic here carefully and precisely because of entanglin and destructive levels of confusion and deceit with regard to this cultural philosophy and psychology of the body. This cultural dynamic is becomin more widespread and ever less acknowledged.

JPII sets us straight in *Familaris Consortio* #11: "Man is called to love in his unified totality. Love includes the human body, and the body is made a sharer in spiritual love." The definition and language of love used by the "sexologists" is a disastrous reduction of the glory of this unified totality of love and the full stature of the human mystery. The whole thing is reduced to the biological factor — a very important factor. As JPII put it, "It is reduced to pure materiality: it is simply a complex of organs, functions and energies to be used according to the sole criteria of pleasure and efficiency." Nevertheless, left alone and separated from the greatness of the fullness of the human person, the body along with the rest of the person is gonna be one incomplete, impoverished, and unhappy person.

B16 in DCE #5 reinforces the totality of this unified dimension and truth of the human person: "It is neither the spirit alone nor the body alone that loves: it is man, the person, a unified creature composed of body and soul, who loves. Only when both dimensions are truly united does man attain his full stature." It's this "full stature" stuff that will effectively combat, defeat, and transform the "impoverished" levels of thinkin feelings and behavior — root causes of much of the unhappiness ragin in the culture and in the lives of so many people. It's this "full stature" stuff that will instruct us how to read and reread the language of our bodies, which are packed with mystery. To unpack this great mystery of the language of love with regard to the body and the full and unified stature of the human person, it's vital to plunge into the fullness of this reality and mystery which involves a philosophy of the body, a psychology of the body, the biology of the body, and the theology of the body — and all of it together at that. If we don't choose to embrace this full approach, the result will be an impoverished and unhappy encounter with "love" — a love that is not great, not fulfillin, not satisfyin, and on and on and on because it's an impoverished love which never satisfies. We will miss out on readin and experiencin the body as a witness to the love that does satisfy.

Learn to read the true language of our bodies packed with mystery.

We must learn to "read" the true language of our bodies. Our bodies proclaim a great mystery. They are not only biological. They are also, and even more so, theological. They speak about who God is, who we are, and who we are called to be. As John Paul II wrote, "This is the body: a witness to creation as a fundamental gift, and therefore, a witness to Love as the source from which this same giving springs. Masculinity — femininity — namely, sex — is the original sign of [God's] creative donation.... This is the meaning with which sex enters into the theology of the body."

— Christopher West, *The Love That Satisfies*, Ascension Press, p. 69

We need the enrichment and transformation of all impoverished reductions of love to the full stature of the human person, and an enrichin encounter with the love that never fails and that satisfies, that makes us happy now and forever, a love that has a "bounce back" capability, so that when we do fail and fall we get aided by the power of the love that satisfies us deeply and at the same time leaves us hungerin for more. Readin the body/the language of love in this way puts us in a better position to see sex speak the language of love, the language that God — who is Love — intended it to be.

As Mary Beth Binachi put it, "Sex is best when it's done God's way. He intended it to speak a language — the language of self-donatin love. The real pleasure comes when we respect the language of sex, when we speak it honestly, in the context in which it belongs" (www.reallove.net, February 8, 2007). This makin a gift of oneself, this language of self-donatin love is connected with the inner need we have to belong. Again, it's not just the biological factor; it's the philosophy, psychology, and the theology of the body. In other words, it's not just about sex. Rather sex, when seen and read on the page of the body as the language of love, it's all about love, the love that includes the whole package because this love is the whole package!

That's why JP/Wojtyla in *Love and Responsibility* says, "Man has an inborn need of betrothed love, a need to give himself to another." Masculinity and femininity become visible signs of truth and love. This new, renewin, and radical readin of the body as the language of love rescues and redeems lust from the destructive, addictive, and impoverishin energies that keep so many people in the bondage of impoverished love.

The body as a sign of truth and love.

The sacramentality of creation and the world was revealed in man created in the image of God. By means of his corporality, his masculinity and femininity man becomes a visible sign of the economy of truth and love, which has its source in God himself.

— JPII, February 20, 1980

Christopher West, in his fine book *The Love That Satisfies* makes an important point about lust. If we don't deal with it with the help of the power of the Redemption — Redemptive

Love — this difficulty with lust could escalate into the ultimate deception, and that is when lust passes itself of as love and we accept it. Check out Christopher: "We must battle against lust if we are to reclaim the freedom that enables us to make a sincere gift of self. This is difficult when lust manifests itself clearly. It is all the more difficult since lust is not always plain and obvious.... Sometimes it is concealed. So that it passes itself off as love." In his book *Theology of The Body for Beginners*, Christopher makes another great point: "As we allow lust to be 'crucified,' we also come to experience the 'resurrection' of God's original plan for sexual desire — not immediately, but gradually, progressively, as we take up our cross every day and follow, we come to experience sexual desire as the power to love in God's image."

Education influenced by culture of relativism affects the body.

Today more than in the past, a person's education and formation are influenced by the messages and climate put across by the media and which are inspired by a mentality and culture of relativism, consumerism and a false and destructive exaltation, or better, profanation, of the body and human sexuality.

— B16, June 11, 2007

Again, that's why JPII spoke of the overwhelmin and inestimable importance of helpin "young people to reflect on these delicate and essential questions, through catechesis and vigorous and suitable talks, making the depth and beauty of human love shine." The reality of all this is more of a challenge now than it was in the past, and as a result, the language of love — the body and human sexuality — suffers more than ever. The nonstop efforts of the media confuse, breakdown, and in some cases even eliminate value and respect with regard to the language of love. The deception resultin from the deliberate confusin of what's fake with what's real and what's real with what's fake is paralyzin. Film and video can now render the wildest fantasies and make them seem realistic. Real events, by the same token, are fictionalized. It's little wonder that the TV generation has a hard time distinguishin between truth and fiction. The impact of this deception is massive in that the media for many is the chief means of information and education.

The nuptual meanin of the body.

This nuptial meaning of the human body can be understood only in the context of the person. The body has a nuptial meaning because the human person, as the Council says, is a creature that God willed for his own sake. At the same time, he can fully discover his true self only in a sincere giving of himself. Christ revealed to man and woman, over and above the vocation to marriage, another vocation namely, that of renouncing marriage, in view of the kingdom of heaven. With this vocation, he highlighted the same truth about the human person. If a man or woman is capable of making a gift of himself for the kingdom of heaven, this proves in its turn (and perhaps even more) that there is the freedom of the gift in the human body. It means that this body possesses a full nuptial meaning.

— JPII, General Audience, January 16, 1980

JP's deep understandin of and experience with the language of love sees a nuptial meaning of the body in marriage as well as in all other vocations in the Church. This is true precisely because this nuptial meaning of the body can be understood only in the context of the full understandin of the human person. There's a huge interconnectedness with the culture of life and love with the language of love: "It is an illusion to think we can build a true culture of human life if we do not ... accept and experience sexuality and love and the whole of life according to their meaning and their close interconnection" (EV #97). Passionately pursuin this close interconnectedness of the language of love with the culture of life and human sexuality will make a major contribution to enrichin all the many and different dimensions of impoverished love.

6. The Great Commandment

love God with everythin and your neighbor as yourself.

Thou shall love the Lord your God with all your heart, and with all your soul, and with all your mind. This is the great and first commandment. And a second is like it; You shall love your neighbor as yourself.

— Matthew 22:38-39

St. Augustine, in his treatise on the Gospel of John, really makes the essence of the great commandment crystal clear:

The Lord, the teacher of love, full of love, came in person with summary judgment on the world, as had been foretold of him, and showed that the law and the prophets are summed up in two commandments of love. . . .

Keep always in mind that we must love God and our neighbor. . . .

These two commandments must always be in your thoughts and in your hearts, treasured, acted on, fulfilled. Love of God is the first to be commanded, but love of neighbor is the first to be put into practice. . . .

Since you do not yet see God, you merit the vision of God by loving your neighbor. By loving your neighbor you prepare your eyes to see God: Saint John says clearly, If you do not love your brother whom you see, how will you love God whom you do not see! (The Liturgy of the Hours, *Vol. I, pp. 511-512*)

I was listenin to the radio the other day, and Reverend Al Sharpton was bein interviewed for some good work he was doin in Harlem. The interviewer revealed that Sharpton was adopted by the late James Brown — the godfather of soul music. Sharpton in turn revealed what he learned about love from his godfather James Brown: "He always taught me that you show love for God by the good you do for others." There it is! The godfather of soul music teachin his godson one of the essential lessons of the precepts of love; in other words, dancin with both feet which gives birth to two wings to fly to heaven!

The 2 precepts of love.

I wish to bind you more closely to myself, by means of love of the neighbor. You know that the precepts of love are two: love of me, and love of the neighbors; in these, as I have testified, consist the Law and the Prophets. I want you to fulfill these two commandments. You must walk, in fact with both feet, not one, and with two wings fly to heaven.

— The Dialogue of St. Catherine of Siena

One of the invaluable lessons to help us learn somethin about love is that charity helps get rid of our selfishness. This process of overcoming, conquering, and transforming our selfishness is a lifelong process connected to the ongoin work of conversion. Gettin rid of our selfishness helps our eyes to be opened and see the needs of our neighbor so we can live and practice love. This puttin love into action makes us sharers in the very love with which we have been loved, which in turn releases the power of love that breaks down walls of isolation.

There is no lack of opportunity to practice charity.

The age in which we live, like every age, is the age of charity. There is certainly no lack of opportunities for practicing it. Every day the media engage our eyes and hearts, bringing us the urgent and desperate appeals of millions of our less fortunate brethren, afflicted by some natural or man-made disaster, those who are hungry, wounded in body or soul, sick, dispossessed, exiled, isolated, and deprived of all help. They reach out to us Christians who wish to love the Gospel and the one great Commandment of Love.

— JPII, Message for Lent, 1986

Then, the buildin-up energies of love will bear abundant fruit by enrichin the lives of others, especially those who are poor and sufferin. Human freedom, as JPII teaches us, reaches its most complete realization by livin the great commandment to love God and neighbor: "In this commandment, human freedom finds its most complete realization — freedom is for love: its realization through love can reach even heroic proportions" (JPII, *Memory and Identity*, p. 44).

Love breaks down walls of isolation.

Charity rids us of our selfishness; it breaks down the walls of our isolation; it opens our eyes to our neighbor, to those more distant from us and to the whole of humanity. Charity is demanding, but it is also heartening, for it is the carrying out of our basic Christian vocation and makes us sharers in the Lord's love.

— JPII, Message for Lent, 1986

Love is the fundamental obligation of the human person towards God and neighbor. This fundamental obligation could very well involve the difficult, painful, and seemingly impossible possibility that this neighbor whom I must love could be an enemy. This great commandment of love could very well even reach heroic proportions; and love makes us free to peruse love on this most important and challengin path. Saint Augustine asks an interesting question: "Does love bring about the keeping of the commandments, or does the keeping of the commandments bring about love? And he answers: But who can doubt that love comes first? For the one who does not love has no reason for keeping the commandments" (cf. JPII, *Veritatis Splendor* #22).

Love embraces everyone, includin enemies.

The love to which the Christian is committed embraces everyone, including enemies. When I was writing the essay "Love and Responsibility," the greatest commandment of the Gospel presented itself to me as a personalist norm. Precisely because man is a personal being, it is not possible to fulfill our duty towards him except by loving him. Just as love is the supreme commandment with regard to the personal God, so too only love can be our fundamental obligation towards the human person, created in God's image and likeness.

— JPII, *Memory and Identity*, p. 150

7. Father of Love

The Father — a fire of love crazy over what he has made.

In your light you saw yourself compelled by the fire of your charity to give us being in spite of the evil we would commit against you, eternal Father. It was fire then that compelled you, oh unutterable love, even though you saw all the evils that your creatures would commit against your infinite goodness, you acted as if you did not see and set your eye only on the beauty of your creature, with whom you have fallen in love, like one drunk and crazy with love.... You concentrated on the love because you are nothing but a fire of love, crazy over what you have made.

— *The Dialogue of St. Catherine of Siena*

The Father's Love is the ultimate and definitive enrichment of our impoverished love. This love of the Father, made visible in Jesus and in his humanity, has become as JPII says, "part of the universe, the human family and history" (JPII encyclical on the Holy Spirit #54). Durin a general audience on Wednesday, July 21, 1999, JPII said, "Since believers are loved in a special way by the Father, they are raised with Christ and made citizens of heaven.... The Fatherhood of God, who is rich in mercy, is experienced by creatures through the love of God's crucified and risen Son, who sits on the right hand of the Father as Lord."

We were loved when we were dead in sin.

God, who is rich in mercy, out of the great love with which he loved us, even when we were dead through our trespasses, made us alive together with Christ (by grace you have been saved), and raised us up with him, and made us sit with him in the heavenly places in Christ Jesus, that in the coming ages he might show the immeasurable riches of his grace in kindness toward us in Christ Jesus.

— Ephesians 2:4-7

We need to be healed by the richness of God's Love.

The world you are inheriting is a world which desperately needs a new sense of brotherhood and human solidarity. It is a world which needs to be touched and healed by the beauty and richness of God's love. It needs witnesses to that love.... It needs you. Do not let hope die! Stake your lives on it! **We are not the sum of our weaknesses and failures; we are the sum of the Father's love for us and our real capacity to become the image of his Son.** *I finish with a final prayer: Lord Jesus Christ keep these young people in your love... Teach them how to profess their faith, bestow their love, and impart their hope to others.*

— JPII, Toronto World Youth Day, July 28, 2002

The tremendous words pourin out of the fatherly heart of JPII at World Youth Day in Toronto 2002 maintain their torrential effect, most especially his amazin conclusion: "We are not the sum of our weaknesses and failures; we are the sum of the Father's love for us and our real capacity to become the image of his son." In other words, the love of the Father empowers us to become livin images of love, in the midst of and in spite of our weaknesses and failures. This fits right in with what JPII said in Rio regardin our participatin with "the full capacity for fulfillment with the Father's loving plan." While on the one hand, this is a huge lesson in learnin somethin about love. On the other hand, this huge lesson is contained in the great basic and foundational prayer Jesus taught us to pray — the Our Father. Most Christians learn this prayer as little children and pray it every day of their lives. Jesus taught us to pray the way he wants us to live, with, in, and through love, the love that the Father has for us, for all, for each and every person on the planet. That's why the Church teaches us in CCC 2792 that "if we pray the Our Father sincerely, we leave individualism behind, because the love that we receive frees us from it."

Jesus makes the Father present as love and mercy, Jesus makes the love of the Father present by his actions and his words. As JPII affirms, in these visible signs of love and mercy through actions and words the Father can be seen. This is another invaluable lesson to help us learn somethin about love — to the degree that we live love and mercy with our words and actions with Jesus, we too make the love of the Father present.

Jesus makes the Father present.

Before His own townspeople, in Nazareth, Christ refers to the words of the prophet Isaiah: "The Spirit of the Lord is upon me, because he has anointed me to preach good news to the poor. He has sent me to proclaim release to the captives and recovering of sight to the blind, to set at liberty those who are oppressed, to proclaim the acceptable year of the Lord." These phrases, according to Luke, are His first messianic declaration. They are followed by the actions and words known through the Gospel. By these actions and words Christ makes the Father present among men. It is very significant that the people in question are especially the poor, those without means of subsistence, those deprived of their freedom, the blind who cannot see the beauty of creation, those living with broken hearts, or suffering from social injustice, and finally sinners. It is especially for these last that the Messiah becomes a particularly clear sign of God who is love, a sign of the Father. In this visible sign the people of our own time, just like the people then, can see the Father.

— JPII, *Rich in Mercy* #3

8. Word of Love

Jesus, the Word of God, is the Word of Love because God is Love. The consequences of this Word are immense and everlastin. For us to be enriched with the fullness this Word of Love reveals and gives to us, it is absolutely essential that we have a correct approach. For this we must look to Jesus. In his book *Jesus of Nazareth*, B16 sees Jesus "in light of his communion with the Father, which is the true center of his personality; without it, we cannot understand him at all, and it is from this center that he makes himself present to us still today" (p. xiv).

Again, let's connect with B16 in his book on Jesus: "Jesus' teaching is not the product of human learning." This point is absolutely indispensable for helpin us grasp the fullness of the truth of love as bein somethin that can't be taught. The Love we're talkin about is not the product of human leanin; but it's absolutely valuable that we use our gift of reason and try to learn somethin about it anyway. So in other words — Love got 2 teach us love. B16 continues teachin us about the teachin of Jesus by pointing out that "it originates from immediate contact with the Father, from 'face-to-face' dialogue — from the vision of the one who rests close to the Father's heart. It is the Son's word." This bein the case, it's the Word of Love that reveals the fullness of the love and mercy from the heart of the Father.

Jesus kindles in the world the fire of God's Love.

He is born in a stable and, coming among us, he kindles in the world the fire of God's love (cf. Lk 12:49). This fire will not be quenched ever again. May this fire burn in our hearts as a flame of charity in action, showing itself in openness to and support of our many brothers and sisters sorely tried by want and suffering! Lord Jesus, whom we contemplate in the poverty of Bethlehem, make us witnesses to your love, that love which led you to strip yourself of divine glory, in order to be born among us and die for us.

— JPII, December 24, 2000, Angelus

Blessed Abbot Marmion, beatified by JPII, is a blessed spiritual theologian. He gives us a great insight into the word of love: "Here below, the love of Jesus for his Father shines out in an ineffable manner. All Christ's life, all his mysteries are summed up in those words which St. John relates, 'I love the Father' (Jn 14:31). Our Lord gave his disciples the infallible criterion of love, 'if you keep my commandments you will abide in my love,' and he at once gave an example, 'As I also have kept my Father's commandments, and abide in his love'" (Jn 15:10, *Fire of Love: An Anthology of Abbot Marmion's Published Writings on The Holy Spirit*, Fr. Charles Dollen, Herder Book Co., St. Louis, p. 16).

The fire burnin in the Word of Love desires to be set ablaze in our hearts through charity in action. This is a love that burns for justice and creates encounters and networks of solidarity with a power that sets limits on evil — cultural, social, political, emotional, and spiritual. We got to do the love; doin the love sets limits upon evil through our overcomin evil in our own lives and in the life of the world by doin good with the power of love. Check out B16 durin Lent of 2006: "In the words of my beloved predecessor, Pope John Paul II, there is a 'divine limit imposed upon evil,' namely mercy." Learnin about this power of love through practicin the spiritual and corporal works of mercy makes an impact in the historical realities of the lives of people with a love that is not sentimental. It's a love that empowers us to make a gift of ourselves trainin us in the school of love which makes sacrifice desirable and doable. It's what B16 said before he became pope: "In the end I just have to drop the question as to what I get out of it. I have to be ready to give myself. I have to learn that it is important to just let myself go…. A part of every human love is that it is only truly great and enriching if I am ready to deny myself, to give of myself. And that is certainly true of our relationship with God, out of which, in the end, all our other relationships must grow."

ℊod's love is not a sentimental love.

God is love; not a sentimental love, but a love that became a total gift to the point of the sacrifice on the Cross.

— B16, January 16, 2007, in a soup kitchen in Rome

The Word of Love penetrates deep into the impoverished life of what EU calls "the jangled and defective life of men." She put it like this: "He was acting as a link between the outpouring of love and harmony of the Life of God and the jangled and defective life of men. 'Tell John the blind see, the lame walk, the lepers are cleansed.' Human life is re-adjusted and made whole by the healing action of dynamic love" (EU, *Anthology*, pp. 59-60). The somethin we can learn about love from the Word of Love is the healin action of love that helps people to feel that they belong. This feelin of belongin is connected with the knowledge of bein definitively and infinitely loved. B16 drove this point home at World Youth Day Cologne: "No one is unwanted. Everyone is loved. Everyone is needed." This dimension of love delivers a fatal blow to impoverished love in all its forms and manifestations. Accordin to Blessed Mother Teresa, feelin unwanted is "the greatest poverty." People feelin unwanted is the great universal impoverisher of love. The Word of Love has been given to be spoken, to be given away and made real in the lives of those who speak this word with their words and actions so the world can know, so that every human person can know that they are loved and are lovable. This does not dismiss the many problems and conflicts with evil whether they be personal, social, institutional, or cultural. Rather, love provides the light and strength of truth for us to choose love and enrich the lives of others.

Nonetheless, the mystery of the Word of Love and the need for this Love to be made real in our lives is a perfect match. God Who is Love wants it done and provides all we need to do it. This is not a trivialization of the evil that works 24/7 to keep people in the impoverishin bondage of thinkin and feelin they are unloved and unlovable. It's a proclamation of the Word of Love that does what it is, the Word is Love and unleashes the power of love so that we can know ourselves as loved, and love with the power of the love that loves us. This is the power and nature of the Word of Love so we can learn to make a more complete gift of ourselves in the unity of love. The perfection of the unity and communion of *eros* and *agape* in the Word of Love, the one movement of love which moves in many different directions according to von B, "is fulfilled in that it sees itself, with all its upward strivings, brought into the service of God's revelation, into the downward movement of his grace and love" (von B, *Explorations in Theology, Vol. I: The Word Made Flesh*, Ignatius Press, 1989, p. 163).

Love created and sustains the ever-expandin universe so that our hearts and minds can also expand by being rooted in the capacity we've been given to love. If we're not engaged and involved in this process, we will wither away in the foul deception of the destructive energies of impoverished love which will slowly destroy and eventually kill us. This is why the great JPII has repeated over and over the important teachin of Vatican II, that it is only in the Mystery of the Word of Love made flesh that we can realize the true greatness of our vocation and of who we are.

Jesus as "love to the end" is not alien to any culture.

Christ, being in truth the incarnate Logos, "love to the end"
is not alien to any culture, nor to any person; on the contrary,
the response that he seeks in the heart of cultures is what
gives them their ultimate identity, uniting humanity and at the
same time expecting the wealth of diversity, opening people
everywhere to growth in genuine humanity, in authentic
progress. The Word of God, in becoming flesh in Jesus Christ,
also became history and culture.

— B16, May 13, 2007

9. Fire of Love

Jesus said, "I came to cast fire upon the earth; and would that it were already kindled!" (Lk 12:49). The Word of Love is burnin with the Fire of Love to set our hearts and lives ablaze with the fire of love. The Holy Spirit — the Spirit of Love — gives and sustains the power of love includin the all-important gift of self-control. The Fire of Love — The Holy Spirit — transforms sufferin into salvific love, creatin a new order of love, pourin love into our hearts that burns to purify and strengthen us to carry pain. All pain, in one way or another, is in some way connected with a rejection of love, which is in some way connected with human weakness and sin. The Spirit of Love forgives our sin and purifies its miserable effects so we can express love, especially through the carryin of the pain of others, and to transform it, relieve it, and give meaning and value to it. In his encyclical on the Holy Spirit JPII testifies that "the Holy Spirit enters into a new and cosmic suffering with a new outpouring of love because of sin.... Sin is understood to be the rejection of love which in turn is the root cause for the suffering of man.... This transforming power is the manifestation of eternal love — the fullness of mercy" (#39).

Love transforms the lover into the one loved.

(Love) is a fire reaching through to the inmost soul. It transforms the lover into the one loved. More deeply, love intermingles with grief, and grief with love, and a certain blending of love and grief occurs. They become so united that we can no longer distinguish love from grief nor grief from love.

Thus the loving heart rejoices in its sorrow and exults in its grieving love.

> — St. Paul of the Cross, *The Liturgy of the Hours*,
> Vol. IV, pp. 1505-1506

In #41 of the same encyclical, JPII refers to the Holy Spirit as "the fire from heaven, which works in the depth of the mystery of the Cross. Here, in the depth of the mystery of the Cross love is at work, that love which brings man back again to share in the life that is in God himself." JPII sees a paradoxical mystery of love in that "in Christ there suffers a God who has been rejected by his own creatures." The Spirit of Love "draws a new measure of the gift" that was given to us at the beginning — the gift of Love. This new measure of the gift of Love from the Spirit of Love restores the love betrayed by Adam, and radically renews us for the radical newness of love. In his last homily as Cardinal Ratzinger before becomin B16 on April 18, 2005, he quotes JPII regardin Jesus and how he "burns and transforms evil through suffering in the fire of his suffering love."

What can we do to have this fire burn and purify us so we can experience this fire of Love? Make frequent and faithful use of the sacraments with the Word of God and the intercession of the Mother of God and all the saints — especially our favorites; grow in knowledge of the faith which comes through hearin the Word of God and rootin ourselves in the tradition and teachins of the Church; and pray, pray, pray with a fervent, faithful, and on-fire interior life. And what do we do when the energy and pull from the conflictin desires within us, and from all the encin yet destructive energies from the culture of death that aim to impoverish and destroy true love hit us hard? Talk to somebody, and be sure that on your somebody list is *that* Somebody — the

Holy Spirit — who, as the Church teaches, "gives new form to our desires" (CCC 2764). JPII talked about — prayed and worked to bring about, and now from the Father's House prays for us to be more and more about — a "new humanity." This new humanity, through the love in the sufferin of Gethsemane — which continues to go on — is a restoration of the Love betrayed by Adam through sin which is one of the really big ongoin sources of this ongoin betrayal of love which keeps love impoverished.

Talkin about befriendin the saints, one of my good friends is St. Thérèse of Lisieux. Thérèse says, "When we cast our faults into the devouring fire of love with total child-like trust, how would they not be consumed so that nothing is left of them?" Growin in love requires growin in trust. As we grow in trust especially by castin our "everything" with total childlike trust into the devourin fire of love, we become protected from growin cold in the midst of the increase of evil. It will also prevent us from slippin into that very dangerous "lukewarm" religion. This lukewarm thing makes Jesus sick to his stomach — literally! In Revelation 3:16 Jesus says, "Because you are lukewarm, and neither cold nor hot, I will spew you out of my mouth." Don't want that to happen! In Mt 24:12 Jesus specifies the increase of evil as the reason for love growin cold: "Because wickedness is multiplied, most men's love will grow cold." No wonder there's not enough of people burnin with more love — the increase of evil sometimes seems to be outmatchin the growin and burnin of love in our lives. We're not matchin the increase of evil with an increase of burnin love.

It is precisely by acceptin the gift of Love that God is and the love that God gives that our freedom is realized to the highest degree. The Fire of Love helps us learn how to integrate "faith working through love" (Gal 5:6). The poverty of our impoverished love becomes enriched by our yearnin for and acceptin the power of love contained in the Fire of the

Love that is God. St. Paul tells us in 2 Corinthians 8:9, "For you know the generous act of our Lord Jesus Christ, that though he was rich, yet for your sakes he became poor, so that by his poverty you might become rich." The Fire of love causes this transformation to be real, enrichin our impoverished love with the fullness and lavishness of the victory of love. This transformative work of love helps us to communicate and live the absolute awesomeness of love right in the midst of it all. "'What no eye has seen, nor ear heard, nor the human heart conceived, what God has prepared for those who love him,' God has revealed to us through the Spirit. For the Spirit searches everything, even the depths of God" (1 Cor 2:9-10).

10. Gift and Mystery

The gift and mystery of Love creates a human solidarity that is so desperately needed and desired by everyone, even when people can't put their finger on what they're feelin and yearnin for. It's possible for love to spring up within us, and even to spring up within us in its fullest degree. The gift and mystery of the Eucharist is both the most powerful and the most mysterious manifestation of this Love that creates and sustains the capacity we have for love and human solidarity. The Eucharist brings about and makes present the Love necessary for this solidarity because it is this love really, truly, and mysteriously present. This solidarity is the foundation of all that is good in each and every culture. It is the source from which flows the love to touch and heal the fragile wounds and unbearable pain of all of us, especially when we feel that we are nothin but the sum of our weaknesses and failures The greatness of JPII at the prayer vigil for World Youth Day in Toronto — July 28, 2002 — is an explosion of the reality of the presence of this Love. His challenge to the youth present, to the youth of the world as well as to every one is immense. He challenged us to be witnesses to the tremendous gift and mystery of this love.

L ove revealed in its fullest degree.

The Sacrament of Love ... the Eucharist signifies this charity, and therefore recalls it, makes it present and at the same time brings it about. Every time that we consciously share in it, there opens in our souls a real dimension of that unfathomable love that includes everything that God has done and continues to do for us human beings, as Christ says: "My Father goes on working, and so do I." Together with this unfathomable and free gift, which is charity revealed in its fullest degree in the saving sacrifice of the Son of God, the sacrifice of which the

Eucharist is the indelible sign, there also springs up within us a lively response of love. We not only know love; we ourselves begin to love. We enter, so to speak, upon the path of love and along this path make progress. Thanks to the Eucharist, the love that springs up within us from the Eucharist develops in us, becomes deeper and grows stronger.

— JPII, *Dominicae Cenae* #5

The solidarity factor of love in the great gift and mystery of the Eucharist makes active love spring up within us and makes it grow stronger. This is made clear by B16 in *Sacramentum Caritatis*: "The Sacrament of charity, the holy Eucharist, is the gift that Jesus Christ makes of himself, thus revealing God's infinite love for every man and woman" (#1). Bein engaged with and commanded by the infinite love that Love has for every man and woman will create somethin radically new. The precise nature of this radical newness is made crystal clear by B16: "This wondrous Sacrament makes manifest that 'greater love'" (SC #1). It's this greater love that enables us to learn somethin about love, and not just with human learnin. We can learn somethin here from the very depths of Love itself. This greater love is what lead Jesus to "lay down his life for his friends" (cf Jn 15:13). We find our greatness in this dimension of the reality of the gift and mystery of Love.

The full deal of the radical newness brought by Christ is in the Eucharist.

There is nothing authentically human — our thoughts and affections, our words and deeds — that does not find in the sacrament of the Eucharist the form it needs to be lived to the full. Here we can see the full human import of the radical newness brought by Christ in the Eucharist: the worship of God in our lives cannot be relegated to something private and individual, but tends by its nature to permeate every aspect of our existence. Worship pleasing to God thus becomes a new way of living our whole life, each particular moment of which is lifted up, since it is lived as part of a relationship with Christ and as an offering to God. The glory of God is the living man (cf. 1 Cor 10:31). And the life of man is the vision of God.... From the beginning Christians were clearly conscious of this radical newness, which the Eucharist brings to human life.

— B16, *Spe Salvi* (SS), 71-72

This radical newness that the gift and mystery of the Eucharist brings to human life is not possible for us to live on our own strength. It's by the gift of the mystery itself that makes us capable for the greatness of this radical newness of love. JPII reminds us in *Veritatis Splendor* #22 that to imitate and live out the love of Christ it "is not possible for man by his own strength alone. He becomes capable of this love only by virtue of a gift received. As the Lord Jesus receives the love of his Father, so he in turn freely communicates that love to his disciples: 'As the Father has loved me, so I have loved you: abide in my love' (Jn 15:9)."

---

*B*efore the gift and mystery we bow low in adoration and unbounded love.

If in the presence of this mystery reason experiences its limits, the heart enlightened by the grace of the Holy Spirit, clearly sees the response that is demanded, and bows low in adoration and unbounded love.

— JPII, *Ecclesia Eucharistia* #6

---

11. The Greatest Mystery

The greatest mystery of love takes us to new and undreamed of places. The richness of our experience of these undreamed of places will depend if, when, and to what degree we surrender and abandon ourselves to the mysterious designs of Love. This is especially true with love and joy, and the development of joy on the path of love. U got 2 love, because it's only when we love that we can be happy. In order to love, you got to make a gift of yourself. Makin a gift of yourself is a radiant manifestation of the highest degree of love — the greatest mystery. Self-givin love for others is such a true and vital dimension of love that JPII declares that heroic actions are actually born from the energy generated when the total gift of self is made.

Everyday heroism — self-giving love for others.

It is in this context, so humanly rich and filled with love, that heroic actions too are born. These are the most solemn celebration of the Gospel of life, for they proclaim it by the total gift of self. They are the radiant manifestation of the highest degree of love, which is to give one's life for the person loved (cf. Jn 15:13). They are a sharing in the mystery of the Cross, in which Jesus reveals the value of every person, and how life attains its fullness in the sincere gift of self. Over and above such outstanding moments, there is an everyday heroism, made up of gestures of sharing, big or small, which build up an authentic culture of life.

— JPII, *Evangelium Vitae* #86

B16 said it plain and clear — "Love gives joy"; but this joy given by love comes at a price. Learnin somethin about how love gives joy in this regard requires us to come out of ourselves, it requires us to lose ourselves. This is both a beautiful and painful process. And yes, this greatest mystery unfolds as the fruit of and in the embrace of Crucified Love. B16, in *Deus Caritas Est* #6, describes love as an "ongoing exodus out of the closed inward looking self towards its liberation through self-giving, and thus towards authentic self-discovery and indeed the discovery of God."

Love is always a process of comin out of oneself.

Love gives joy. But love is always a process of losing oneself, hence, a process of coming out of oneself; in this regard, it is also a painful process. Only in this way is it beautiful and helps us to mature and to attain true joy....This joy however, only develops on the path of love, and this path of love has to do with the Cross, with communion with the Crucified Christ.

— B16, March 2, 2007

St. Basil of Caesarea was quoted by St. Gregory Nazianzen when he preached at Basil's funeral: "The human being is an animal who has received the vocation to become God." To become God — to become love, the greatest dimension of the vocation of every human person rooted in the greatest mystery of all mysteries, the mystery of Love. One of the greatest things about the greatest mystery of Love is that it imposes a divine limit upon evil. Accordin to JPII, love is mercy's second name, and it is mercy that imposes this divine limit on evil. This divine limit imposed on evil occurs in the mystery of the redemption: "If redemption marks the divine limit placed upon evil, it is for this reason only: because thereby evil is radically overcome by good, hate by love, death by resurrection" (*Memory and Identity*, pp. 23-24).

By lovin Jesus we can transform history.

It is only by knowing, loving and imitating Christ that, with him, we can transform history, by bringing gospel values to bear in society and culture.

— JPII, to U.S. Bishops, June 4, 2004

The greatest mystery of love contains within itself the fullness of the original vocation to love, which belongs to every person on the planet. The greatness of the vocation of man is rooted in the sincere and total gift of self. So great is the love of Jesus on the Cross that his blood becomes the powerful means for the enrichment of the world with a mysterious and real communion of love. In *Evangelium Vitae* #25, JPII clarifies this point: "Precisely because it is poured out as the gift of life, the blood of Christ is no longer a sign of death, of definitive separation from the brethren, but the instrument of a communion which is richness of life for all. Whoever in the Sacrament of the Eucharist drinks this blood and abides in Jesus (cf. Jn 6:56) is drawn into the dynamism of his love and gift of life, in order to bring to its fullness the original vocation to love which belongs to everyone (cf. Gen 1:27; 2:18-24)."

In this greatest mystery, human dignity is redeemed from all that can impoverish our learnin, understandin, experiencin, and practicin love. B16 said Jesus "truly becomes food for us — as love" (DCE #13). This is for sure an expression of the greatest mystery which expands our possibilities, makin us capable for greater good and more love; and at the same time, it doesn't get any simpler than Jesus becomin for us food — as love.

Love totally fulfilled and open to new horizons.

The story of each soul is that of a love which is totally fulfilled, and at the same time open to new horizons, because God continually expands the possibilities of the soul, so as to make it capable of ever greater good.

— B16, September 4, 2007

12. God Is Love

God is love.

Beloved, let us love one another; for love is of God, and he who loves is born of God and knows God. He who does not love does not know God; for God is love.

— 1 John 4:7-8

In light of the truth that God is Love, the divine law of love becomes indispensable for the ultimate fulfillment of love in the world. Love is the ultimate source of fulfillment which alone is able to enrich and transform all and every manifestation of impoverished love. God is love, and every person is loved by God. As a result of this truth, JPII has a deep and burnin conviction that the proclamation "Man is loved by God" is owed to humanity by the Church. JPII specifically and passionately passes this fire on to the youth of the world and to everybody! That humanity is loved by God is to be proclaimed by the words and deeds of Christians through their passionate pursuit of Christ openin wide the doors of their hearts to him.

Humanity is loved by God.

Opening wide the doors to Christ, accepting him into humanity itself poses absolutely no threat to persons, indeed it is the only road to take to arrive at the total truth and the exalted value of the human individual. This vital synthesis will be achieved when the lay faithful know how to put the gospel and their daily duties of life into a most shining and convincing testimony, where, not fear but the loving pursuit of Christ and adherence to him will be the factors determining how a person is to live and grow, and these will lead to new ways of living more in conformity with human dignity. Humanity is loved by God! This very simple yet profound proclamation is owed to humanity by the Church. Each Christian's words and life must make this proclamation resound: God loves you, Christ came for you, Christ is for you "the Way, the Truth and the Life!"

— John 14:6

In the gradual unfoldin of this encounter with God who is love, we have to work hard and be committed to rememberin that love is not merely a sentiment. Sentiments come and go. B16 reminds us that "a sentiment can be a marvelous first spark, but it is not the fullness of love" (DCE #17). Movin beyond the sentiment of love, which has a place, to the all-embracin and all-demandin fullness of love is quite a move; the journey into the fullness of love is blazin fire. In a letter to one of her Dominican brothers, St. Catherine of Sienna expressed her desire for him to be set on fire, swallowed up and consumed in the blazin charity of God who is love. She saw the blazin fire of love as a peaceful sea which she discovered in the words "God is love." JPII sees Jesus, the Love of God in the flesh, as kindlin in the world the fire of God who is Love.

---

*G*od is love — a peaceful sea of blazin charity.

I long to see you set afire, swallowed up and consumed in his blazing charity, for we know that those who are set afire and consumed in that true charity lose all self-consciousness. That is what I want you to do. I am inviting you in this blazing charity to plunge into a peaceful sea, a deep sea. I have rediscovered the sea in the words "God is love".... These words echo within me that everything that is done is simply love, because everything is made entirely of love. This is why he says "I am God, Love."

— St. Catherine of Siena,
Letter to Frate Tomoso Della Fonte

Enterin into this blazin charity is the fruit of intimacy, which will increase the awareness of and commitment to communion and solidarity with others. The more we cling to Jesus and burn with the fire of his Love, the closer we will become to others.

Enter into the intimacy of love.

The more you cling to Jesus the more capable you will become of being close to one another; and insofar as you make concrete gestures of reconciliation you will enter into the intimacy of his love.... God is love; every person is loved by God, who expects to be welcomed and loved by each one. This is a message, young people of today, that you are called to receive and to shout aloud to those of your own age: "Man is loved by God"! This very simple yet profound proclamation is owed to humanity by the Church.

— JPII, Message for 12th World Youth Day

As B16 points out, the first initiative of the Love that loved us first can ignite a spark of response within us that is not just one of feelings. A real and responsible response of love can blossom within us: "We experience the love of God, we perceive his presence and we thus learn to recognize that presence in our daily lives. He has loved us first and he continues to do so; we too, then, can respond with love. God does not demand of us a feeling which we ourselves are incapable of producing. He loves us, he makes us see and experience his love, and since he has 'loved us first,' love can also blossom as a response within us" (B16, DCE #17).

We are not capable of producin a response, a full response, to the love and fire of God within us: "Just as a stone does not fall by its own activity but by the gravitational pull of the earth, so we do not fall in God as a result of what we ourselves try to do. We become the persons we really are solely by the gravitational pull of the love with which God infinitely and unconditionally loves us" (*The Footprints of Love*, Hein Blommestijn, Jos Huls, Kees Waaijman, trans. John Vriend Peters, 2000, Leurven, p. 19). The authors of *Footprints* ask a great question: "What does it mean to admit the love of God and to fall in love with the love with which God loves us?" (p. 19) The followin answer from Jacques Maritain helps us learn somethin about love: "God loves us by making us participate in his nature by grace — by making the sanctified soul his dwelling" (Jacques Maritain, *Notebooks*, Maji Books, Inc., 1984, p. 221). I love the followin from my tragic hero Vincent van Gogh: "You must not be astonished when, even at the risk of you taking me for a fanatic, I tell you that in order to love, I think it is absolutely necessary to believe in God.... To me, to believe in God is to feel that there is a God, not dead or stuffed but alive, urging us to love again with irresistible force — that is my opinion" (Vincent van Gogh, Letter 161).

This openin of the heart to love will prepare the world for a more intense and generous response to the needs of community — family, friends, and strangers — to the lovin and expandin sense of fraternity: "The fire of divine love feeds that of fraternal love.... It is impossible to spread the generating fire of love among others if one has not been inwardly moved by divine love" (JPII, May 18, 1998). This fire within will make our capacity for love authentic; it will make the fundamental human vocation to love real and fruitful — we will become lovin people and as such, authentic images of God.

The vocation to love makes the human person an authentic image of God.

The debasement of human love, the suppression of the authentic capacity for loving, is turning out in our time to be the most suitable and effective weapon to drive God away from men and women, to distance God from the human gaze and heart....It is the vocation to love that makes the human person an authentic image of God. Man and woman come to resemble God to the extent that they become loving people.

— B16, June 6, 2005, to the Ecclesial Diocesan
Convention of Rome

On October 2, 1985, JPII assured us that in light of and in spite of all our struggles with evil, the force and power of love is so great it can help us learn how to draw forth good from evil, renewin and sustainin us with new life: "The truth that God is love constitutes the apex of all that has been revealed.... Love remains as the expression of omnipotence (= unlimited power and authority) in the face of evil, in the face of sin. Only omnipotent love can draw forth good from evil and new life from sin and death."

The inner accomplishin of the law of divine love.

This law of divine love accomplishes in a person four things that are much to be desired. First, it is the cause of one's spiritual life. For it is evident that by the very nature of the action what is loved is in the one who loves. Therefore whoever loves God possesses God in himself; for Scripture says,

"Whoever remains in love remains in God and God in him."
*It is the nature of love to transform the lover into the object
loved. And so if we love God, we ourselves become divinized;
for again, "Whoever is joined to God becomes one spirit with
him." Augustine adds, "As the soul is the life of the body, so
God is the life of the soul." Thus the soul acts virtuously and
perfectly when she acts through charity, and through charity
God lives in her; indeed, without charity she cannot act; for
Scripture says, "Whoever does not love, remains in death."*

— St. Thomas Aquinas (*Opuscula, In duo praecenta*, ed. J.P. Tor-
rel, in Revue des Sc. Phil. Et Théol., 69, 1985, pp. 26-29)

Love presses a new value and orientation on human life.

*We have believed in love: this is the essence of Christianity.
Therefore, our liturgical assembly today must focus on this
essential truth, on the love of God, capable of impressing an
absolutely new orientation and value on human life. Love is
the essence of Christianity, which makes the believer and the
Christian community a leaven of hope and peace in every
environment and especially attentive to the needs of the poor
and needy.*

— B16, September 23, 2007

13. Who Is My Neighbor?

Gaudium et Spes #22 is one of the consistent points of reference in the teachings of JPII: "By his incarnation the Son of God has united himself in some fashion with every human being. This saving event reveals to humanity not only the boundless love of God who 'so loved the world that he gave his only Son' (Jn 3:16), but also the incomparable value of every human person" (JPII, EV #2).

The fullest meanin of the commandment from a lovin heart.

Jesus brings God's commandments to fulfillment, particularly the commandment of love of neighbor, by interiorizing their demands and by bringing out their fullest meaning. Love of neighbor springs from a loving heart which, precisely because it loves, is ready to live out the loftiest challenges. Jesus shows that the commandments must not be understood as a minimum limit not to be gone beyond, but rather as a path involving a moral and spiritual journey towards perfection, at the heart of which is love (cf. Col 3:14). Thus the commandment "You shall not murder" becomes a call to an attentive love which protects and promotes the life of one's neighbor. The precept prohibiting adultery becomes an invitation to a pure way of looking at others, capable of respecting the spousal meaning of the body: "You have heard that it was said to the men of old, 'You shall not kill; and whoever kills shall be liable to judgment.' But I say to you that every one who is angry with his brother shall be liable to judgment.... You have heard that it was said, 'You shall not commit adultery.' But I say to you that every one who looks at a woman lustfully has already committed adultery with her in his heart" (Mt 5:21-22, 27-28). Jesus himself is the living "fulfillment" of the Law inasmuch as he fulfils its authentic meaning by the total gift of himself: he himself becomes a living and personal Law, who invites people to follow him; through the Spirit, he gives the grace to share his own life and love and provides the strength to bear witness to that love in personal choices and actions (cf. Jn 13:34-35).

— JPII, *Veritatis Splendor* #12

On June 22, 1963, in his first message to the human family, titled *"Qui fausto Die"* Pope Paul VI connected love of neighbor as bein proof for love of God. He had the grandeur of vision, due to his heart expanded by love, to see the global proportions of the demands of love and justice; to see the remedy as a response to the demands of love in the "sweet light of charity and mutual collaboration." This mutual workin together in the vision of the great JPII has the center of its scope sighted on the neighbor; it requires communion and solidarity. This communion, as JPII said, is not merely in the life of the Church; it's a project of solidarity for all humanity. This communion and solidarity will not only result in "intimate union with God but also the unity of the whole human race" (JPII, *Stay with Us Lord* #27). So we're talkin about one "big neighbor" here.

L ove of neighbor is proof of love of God.

The unequivocal order of love of neighbor, the proof of the love of God, demands from all men a more equitable solution of the social problems; it demands provisions and cures for developing countries, where often the standard of life is not worthy of the human person; it imposes a global study to improve the conditions of life. This new era, which has been opened to humanity through the conquests of space, will be blessed by the Lord if men learn how to recognize each other as brothers not competitors, to build a world order in holy reverence of God, respecting his Law, in the sweet light of charity and mutual collaboration.

— Pope Paul VI, *Qui Fausto Die*

While in Vienna on September 11, 2007, B16 talked about a culture of volunteerism: "Volunteer work is really about the heart of the Christian image of God and man: love of God and love of neighbor." He continued, "It is good to meet people who are trying to give a face to the Gospel message in our communities; to see people, young and old, who concretely express in Church and society the love which we, as Christians, must be overwhelmed: the love of God which enables us to see others as our neighbors, our brothers and sisters!"

Volunteer work reflects the love we have received.

Volunteer work reflects gratitude for, and the desire to share with others, the love that we ourselves have received. In the words of the fourteenth-century theologian Duns Scotus, "Deus vult condiligentes" — God wants persons who love together with him. Seen in this light, unremunerated service has much to do with God's grace. A culture which would calculate the cost of everything, forcing human relationships into a strait jacket of rights and duties, is able to realize, thanks to the countless people who freely donate their time and service to others, that life is an unmerited gift. For all the many different or even contradictory reasons which motivate people to volunteer their services, all are ultimately based on a profound solidarity born of "gratuitousness." It was as a free gift that we received life from our Creator, it was as a free gift that we were set free from the blind alley of sin and evil, it was as a free gift that we were given the Spirit with his many gifts.

In my Encyclical I wrote: "Love is free; it is not practiced as a way of achieving other ends" (DCE #31).

— B16, Vienna, September 11, 2007

There are people who see, but pretend not to see, who are faced with human needs yet remain indifferent. This is part of the coldness of our present time. In the gaze of others, and particularly of the person who needs our help, we experience the concrete demands of Christian love. Jesus Christ does not teach us a spirituality "of closed eyes," but one of "alertness," one which entails an absolute duty to take notice of the needs of others and of situations involvin those whom the Gospel tells us are our neighbors.

Love of neighbor always involves a voluntary commitment.

Love of neighbor is not something that can be delegated; the State and the political order, even with their necessary concern for the provision of social services, — as you, Mr. President, have said — cannot take its place. Love of neighbor always demands a voluntary personal commitment, and the State, of course, can and must provide the conditions which make this possible. Thanks to such involvement, assistance maintains a human dimension and does not become depersonalized. Volunteers like yourselves, then, are not "stopgaps" in the social fabric, but people who truly contribute to giving our society a humane and Christian face.

— B16, Vienna, September 11, 2007

The gaze of Jesus, what "his eyes" teach us about love, leads to human closeness, solidarity, givin time, sharin our gifts and even our material goods. For this reason, "those who work for the Church's charitable organizations must be distinguished by the fact that they do not merely meet the needs of the moment — as important as this is — but they dedicate themselves to others with heartfelt concern.... This heart sees where love is needed, and acts accordingly" (B16, DCE #31). In his book on Jesus, B16 takes it ever further, pressin with the radical newness of love: "I have to become like someone in love, someone whose heart is open to being shaken up by another's need. Then I find my neighbor or — better — then I am found by him" (*Jesus of Nazareth*, New York, 2007, p. 194). Wow! To have my heart open to the point of bein "shaken up" by the need of someone else! What love! That's why u got 2 love, because if you don't, you'll miss that shakin of your heart, you'll miss out on the fullness of love. You won't live every day "like someone in love." Imagine!

---

l ove is the fulfillment of the law.

A stranger is no longer a stranger for the person who must become a neighbor to someone in need, to the point of accepting responsibility for his life, as the parable of the Good Samaritan shows so clearly (cf. Lk 10:25-37). Even an enemy ceases to be an enemy for the person who is obliged to love him (cf. Mt 5:38-48; Lk 6:27-35), to "do good" to him (cf. Lk 6:27, 33, 35) and to respond to his immediate needs promptly and with no expectation of repayment (cf. Lk 6:34-35). The height of this love is to pray for one's enemy. By so doing we achieve harmony with the providential love of God: "But I say to you, love your enemies and pray for those who persecute you, so that you may be children of your Father who is in heaven; for he makes his sun rise on the evil and on the good and sends rain on the just and on the unjust" (Mt 5:44-45; cf. Lk 6:28, 35). Thus the deepest element of God's commandment to protect human life is the requirement to show reverence and love for every person and the life of every person. This is the teaching which the Apostle Paul, echoing the words of Jesus, addresses to the Christians in Rome: "The commandments, You shall not commit adultery, You shall not kill, You shall not steal, You shall not covet," and any other commandment, are summed up in this sentence, "You shall love your neighbor as yourself." Love does no wrong to a neighbor; therefore love is the fulfilling of the law (Rom 13:9-10).

— JPII, *Evangelium Vitae* #41

14. Eros and Agape

Eros and *agape* have a long, long history. A piece of that history, from the Catholic point of view, has seen *eros* as "bad" because of the connection between *eros* and the "erotic" (= devoted to, or tending to arouse sexual love or desire; strongly marked or affected by sexual desire). Some scholars have charged Christianity with the destruction of *eros*. B16 sheds radiant light on this fallacy. His encyclical *Deus Caritas Est* is an epic masterpiece of comprehensive clarity with regard to settin things straight and helpin us learn somethin about love with regard to *eros* and *agape*. In #5, B16 declares it is neither the spirit alone nor the body alone that loves: it is man, the person, a unified creature composed of body and soul, who loves. Only when both dimensions are truly united, does man attain his full stature. Only thus is love — *eros* — able to mature and attain its authentic grandeur. The full authentic grandeur of love sometimes manifests itself through "sublimation." To sublimate means to divert the expression of instinctual desire or impulse from unacceptable forms to a form that is considered more socially or culturally acceptable. In other words, it's another way of learnin somethin about the unity of love in *eros* and *agape*.

In #8 of DCE, B16 makes the followin claim: "Fundamentally, 'love' is a single reality, but with different dimensions; at different times, one or other dimension may emerge more clearly. Yet when the two dimensions are totally cut off from one another, the result is a caricature or at least an impoverished form of love." The effect of an impoverished form of love restricts and even prevents the true nature of love, the fullness of love to be lived in our lives blossomin into the full stature of the human person; rather than enrichment through true love, we end up with impoverishment through false love. The tragic impoverishment of *eros* can never help us access and develop our capacity for the fullness of love (cf. DCE #7).

$\mathcal{E}$ros and *agape* can never be completely separated.

Eros *and* agape — *ascending love and descending love* — *can never be completely separated. The more the two, in their different aspects, find a proper unity in the one reality of love, the more the true nature of love in general is realized. Even if* eros *is at first mainly covetous and ascending, a fascination for the great promise of happiness, in drawing near to the other, it is less and less concerned with itself, increasingly seeks the happiness of the other, is concerned more and more with the beloved, bestows itself and wants to "be there for" the other. The element of* agape *thus enters into this love, for otherwise* eros *is impoverished and even loses its own nature.*

— B16, *Deus Caritas Est* #7

Christopher West helps us learn somethin about love with regard to us takin stock on our willingness to practice renunciation, sacrifice, and discipline: "This tragic impoverishment of *eros* can never satisfy the longings of the human heart. But are men and women willing to pay the price of renunciation, sacrifice, and discipline required to find and live the love that does satisfy? The answer to this question will determine the entire course of a person's life" (*The Love That Satisfies*, p. 19). This determination will prevent *eros* from losin the radical dimension of its nature, which is always orientated towards fullness. The reality of this fullness of love is far greater and far beyond what we experience every day. While inspiration and instinct have major roles to play, they are not enough. Instinct and inspiration must be complemented with purification and renunciation. In this way, *eros* is not poisoned or rejected, but rather *eros* is healed and restored to its true greatness, enrichin love with the radical newness that orientates love towards its fullness.

Eros and the path of renunciation.

Love promises infinity, eternity — a reality far greater and totally other than our everyday existence. Yet we have also seen that the way to attain this goal is not simply by submitting to instinct. Purification and growth in maturity are called for; and these also pass through the path of renunciation. Far from rejecting or "poisoning" eros, they heal it and restore its true grandeur.

— B16, *Deus Caritas Est* #5

The birth of selfless love is rooted in the union of *eros* and *agape*. *Eros* becomes "less and less concerned with itself and is concerned more and more with the beloved, bestows itself and wants to 'be there for' the other. The element of *agape* thus enters into this love" (DCE #6). This love will also manifest material help — food, clothin, shelter, and all the corporal and spiritual works of mercy. "Seeing with the eyes of Christ, I can give to others much more than their outward necessities, I can give them the look of love, which they crave" (DCE #18). This birth of selfless love impacts the big picture with the reality of the fullness of love explodin with deeds of love. The transformation of *eros* into charity generates the energies of love that affect one's immediate family and the larger families of society, culture, the Church, and the world. It awakens the spiritual energy necessary for the work of justice, penetratin the reality of the world, of history, and all cultures with love.

Acceptin God's love is not enough.

One could rightly say that the revelation of God's eros toward man is, in reality, the supreme expression of His agape. In all truth, only the love that unites the free gift on oneself with the impassioned desire for reciprocity instills a joy, which eases the heaviest of burdens. Jesus said; "When I am lifted up from the earth, I will draw all men to myself" (Jn 12:32). The response the Lord ardently desires of us is above all that we welcome His love and allow ourselves to be drawn to Him. Accepting His love, however, is not enough. We need to respond to such love and devote ourselves to communicating it to others. Christ "draws me to Himself" in order to unite Himself to me, so that I learn to love ... with His own love.

— B16, Lent, 2007

In his Lenten message for 2007, B16 uttered perhaps one of his most radical statements with regard to *eros* and *agape*. The complete unity and inseparability of *eros* and *agape* was put forth with that unique and amazin "B-six-tinnian" clarity. He said that we could rightly say that "the revelation of God's *eros* toward man, is in reality, the supreme expression of His *agape*." The whole point of this revelation is to have us burn with this love and move beyond the acceptin of it, so we can learn to love with the very love with which we have been loved. In footnote 7 of DCE #9, B16 dips deep into Church history to confirm his point that love can certainly be called *eros*, and that love is totally *agape*. In footnote 7, he refers to Dionysius the Areopagite who calls God both *eros* and *agape*.

God is a lover with all the passion of a true love.

God is the absolute and ultimate source of all being; but this universal principle of creation — the Logos, primordial reason — is at the same time a lover with all the passion of a true love. Eros is thus supremely ennobled, yet at the same time it is so purified as to become one with agape. We can thus see how the reception of the Song of Songs in the canon of sacred Scripture was soon explained by the idea that these love songs ultimately describe God's relation to man and man's relation to God. Thus the Song of Songs became, both in Christian and Jewish literature, a source of mystical knowledge and experience, an expression of the essence of biblical faith: that man can indeed enter into union with God — his primordial aspiration. But this union is no mere fusion, a sinking in the nameless ocean of the Divine; it is a unity which creates love, a unity in which both God and man remain themselves and yet become fully one. As Saint Paul says: "He who is united to the Lord becomes one spirit with him" (1 Cor 6:17).

— B16, *Deus Caritas Est* #10

In addition to purifyin and elevatin the "erotic," *eros* and *agape* continue marchin on, wieldin the energies of love, embracing "libido" — the psychic energy derived from the basic biological urges; plain and simple, it's the stuff that makes up sexual drive. The purifyin and elevatin energies of love transform libido into what psychology calls affective energy. Lepp points out that "the same psychic energy nourishes the erotic love between a man and a woman, filial, paternal, and fraternal love, the love of science, of art, of philosophy, friendship, and even the mystical love of God" (Lapp, *The*

Psychology of Loving, p. 195). Affective energy is another expression of the reality of the unity of *eros* and *agape*.

Eros, *agape*, and sublimated love.

Frequently, art, ideas, an ideal, science, one's country, humanity, or God constitutes the object of our love. These can be loved just as much (and at the same time) as a wife or a friend. Certain men actually love one or another of these "higher values" even more than they love a wife, a friend, or their own life. There are countless numbers of persons who would gladly give their lives for their country. Others sacrifice an entire life to science or art, and the list of those who have been martyrs for their religion is a very long one.... Psychoanalysis calls such forms of preferential (if not exclusive) love for realities of a sublimated character sublimated love.... It is permissible for the man of faith to believe that in addition to talent and genius, the grace of God can act to direct affective energy toward the heights, putting it at the disposal, for example, of mystical experience.

— Lepp, *The Psychology of Loving*, pp. 211-12

This whole expression of the energy of "mad *eros*" does not allow those burnin with love to remain closed-up and restricted in themselves, but moves them to become one with the one they love. It's also seen in the symbolic gestures that spontaneously erupt deep in the poetic temperaments of those burnin with this "mad *eros*." Jacques Maritain along with JPII and B16 refers to a "mad boundless love" that spontaneously springs up from the depths of the soul makin a transition from the "regime" or the regular customary way of doin things, to this more explosive spontaneous way of doin things with the passion of a great love combines with what he calls the absolute liberty of the spirit of God.

The regime of mad boundless love.

Who knows if some day mad, boundless love for God will not surge up from the depth of their soul with an irresistible force to take control of how they govern themselves, so that they find themselves brought from the regime of friendship to the regime of mad boundless love? Everything depends in these things on the liberty of the Spirit of God, which is an absolute liberty — and which can cause anyone, whatever his state of life may be, to pass under the regime of the gifts.

— Jacques Maritain, *Notebooks*, p. 239

B16 sees the boundless love of this "mad *eros*" expressed in God Himself: "On the Cross, God's *eros* for us is made manifest." The greatness of God's passionate love for his people is seen in the mystery of the Cross, which unleashes the power of love that forgives. In DCE #10, B16 sees the greatness of this love as so great that God — who is Love — turns against his justice: "God's passionate love for his people — for humanity — is at the same time a forgiving love. It is so great that it turns God against himself, his love against his justice. Here Christians can see a dim prefigurement of the mystery of the Cross: so great is God's love for man that by becoming man he follows him even into death, and so reconciles justice and love."

15. Forgiveness

Forgiveness demonstrates love more powerful than sin.

Society can become "ever more human" only when we introduce into all the mutual relationships which form its moral aspect the moment of forgiveness, which is so much of the essence of the Gospel. Forgiveness demonstrates the presence in the world of the love which is more powerful than sin. Forgiveness is also the fundamental condition for reconciliation, not only in the relationship of God with man, but also in relationships between people. A world from which forgiveness was eliminated would be nothing but a world of cold and unfeeling justice.... For this reason, the Church must consider it one of her principal duties — at every stage of history and especially in our modern age — to proclaim and to introduce into life the mystery of mercy, supremely revealed in Jesus Christ. Not only for the Church herself as the community of believers but also in a certain sense for all humanity, this mystery is the source of a life different from the life which can be built by man, who is exposed to the oppressive forces of the threefold concupiscence active within him. It is precisely in the name of this mystery that Christ teaches us to forgive always. How often we repeat the words of the prayer which He Himself taught us, asking "forgive us our trespasses as we forgive those who trespass against us," which means those who are guilty of something in our regard.... Christ emphasizes so insistently the need to forgive others that when Peter asked Him how many times he should forgive his neighbor He answered with the symbolic number of "seventy times seven," meaning that he must be able to forgive everyone every time.... The Church rightly considers it her duty and the purpose of her mission to guard the authenticity of forgiveness, both in life and behavior and in educational and pastoral work. She protects it simply by guarding its source, which is the mystery of the mercy of God Himself as revealed in Jesus Christ.

— JPII, *Rich in Mercy* #14

In CCC 2843, the Church draws upon the love necessary for forgiveness by linkin forgiveness with the love that "loves to the end" (cf. *Jn* 13:1). By doin so, *forgiveness becomes a living reality.* If we stay within the gaze of Love, there is no escapin forgiveness. If we stay within the gaze of love, forgiveness is possible. Livin love by offerin forgiveness, and allowin ourselves to be forgiven, is one of the most if not "the most" powerful acts we can accomplish that renders us most like unto God who is Love.

Forgivin another human being who has hurt us is somethin that's not possible for us without bein rooted and connected in some way in the fullness of Love. If and when we surrender our hearts to the Spirit of Love — the Holy Spirit — He turns guilt, shame, and all the impoverished stuff we feel with regard to not bein able to forgive those who hurt us into feelings of compassion and intercession. So in other words, we line up our feelings with the feelings of the other person, which in turn takes the focus off ourselves. When we turn to love with a cry that opens our hearts wide to expand with the power of Love, it is only then that we'll have love poured into our hearts which will not disappoint us, but will rather give us livin hope of bein able to love and experience forgiveness in its fullness. This is so, as the Church teaches, because forgiveness "bears witness that, in our world, love is stronger than sin" (CCC 2844). JPII says basically the same thing in his encyclical on Mercy #14: "Forgiveness demonstrates the presence in the world of the love which is more powerful than sin."

It is not in our power.

Thus the Lord's words on forgiveness, the love that loves to the end (cf. Jn 13:1), become a living reality. The parable of the merciless servant, which crowns the Lord's teaching on ecclesial communion, ends with these words: "So also my heavenly Father will do to every one of you, if you do not forgive your brother from your heart" (cf. Mt 18:23-35). It is there, in fact, "in the depths of the heart," that everything is bound and loosed. It is not in our power not to feel or to forget an offense; but the heart that offers itself to the Holy Spirit turns injury into compassion and purifies the memory in transforming the hurt into intercession.

— CCC 2843

The injury and guilt inflicted on people through the hardships of life and the failures of love are themselves injuries to truth and to love. B16, in *Jesus of Nazareth*, says that "God is a God who forgives, because he loves his creatures; but forgiveness can only penetrate and become effective in one who is himself forgiving" (p. 157). So, in other words, "u got 2 forgive." It's the "forgive us as we forgive" petition Jesus taught us in the Our Father. Nonetheless, the destruction caused by the hardships of life and the failures of love need to be repaired.

B16 points out that forgiveness is more than denyin, ignorin, or plain old tryin to forget what happened. There's a whole bunch of destructive things people wind up doin to themselves to shake the pain. Only Love strengthens us to carry pain, our own pain and the pain of others. However, "Guilt must be worked through, healed, and thus overcome. Forgiveness exacts a price — first of all from the person who forgives. He must overcome within himself the evil done to him; as it were, burn it interiorly and in doing so renew himself" (B16, *Jesus of Nazareth*, pp. 158-159).

Work through and suffer through evil by means of love.

The petition for forgiveness is more than a moral exhortation —
though it is that as well, and as such it challenges us anew every
day.... It reminds us of he who allowed forgiveness to cost
him descent into the hardship of human existence, and death
on the Cross. It calls us first and foremost to thankfulness for
that, and then, with him, to work through and suffer through
evil by means of love. And while we must acknowledge day by
day how little our capacities suffice for the task, and how often
we ourselves keep falling into guilt, this petition gives us the
great consolation that our prayer is held safe within the power
of his love — with which, through which, and in which it can
still become a power of healing.

— B16, *Jesus of Nazareth*, p. 160

There are many great stories about love and forgiveness in Desert Fathers. Here's one of them: "An old man was asked, 'What is humility?' He replied, 'It is when your brother sins against you and you forgive him before he comes to ask for forgiveness'" (*Wisdom of the Desert Fathers*, Benadicta Ward, SLG Press, 1997, p. 48, #171). By thinking this kind of love is how we gradually overcome our pride. St. John Chrysostom has an amazing insight regardin the sin and guilt of St. Peter; he has this thing he calls *God's dispensation*: "God's plan permitted Peter to sin ... because he was entrusted with the whole people of God, and sinlessness added to his severity might have made him unforgiving toward his brothers and sisters. He fell into sin so that, remembering his own fault and the Lord's forgiveness, he might forgive others out of love for them" (*Magnificat*, Vol. 9, No. 7/September 2007, p. 168).

Holiness increases our capacity for conversion.

Holiness does not consist in never having erred or sinned. Holiness increases the capacity for conversion, for repentance, for willingness to start again and, especially, for reconciliation and forgiveness.... There are also disputes, disagreements and controversies among saints. And I find this very comforting, because we see that the saints have not "fallen from heaven." They are people like us, who also have complicated problems.... Consequently, it is not the fact that we have never erred but our capacity for reconciliation and forgiveness.

— B16, January 31, 2007, General Audience

On April 2, 1998, exactly six years before he would go to the Father's House, JPII met with a group of young people in Rome. Durin this gatherin he referred to the Cross as the first letter of God's alphabet and made a connection of the love and forgiveness that flows from the Cross with the life of every person. He even spelled "Roma" backwards which gives the word "amor" which is Italian for love. Talk about torrential love and a big heart greatly expanded by love for the greatness of love and forgiveness:

The Cross is concealed in the very name of Rome. If we read Roma (Rome) backwards, we say the word "Amor." Is not the Cross the message of the love of Christ, of the Son of God, who loved us to the point of being nailed to the wood of the Cross? Yes, the Cross is the first letter in God's alphabet. Just as it is not foreign to Rome, the Cross is not foreign to the life of every man and woman of any age, people or social condition.... Yes, the Cross is written into man's life. Wanting to exclude it from one's own life is like wanting to ignore the reality of the human condition. This is how it is! We are made for life, yet we cannot eliminate suffering and trials from our personal experience. And you too, dear young people, do you not experience the reality of the Cross every day? Then when there is no peace in the family, when it becomes difficult to study, when sentiments are not reciprocated, when it is almost impossible to find work, when plans for having a family have to be delayed for financial reasons, when you must contend with illness, loneliness and when there is a risk of falling prey to a dangerous emptiness of values, is it not the Cross that challenges you?

A widespread culture of the ephemeral, which gives value only to what appears beautiful and gives pleasure, would like to make you believe that the Cross should be removed. This cultural trend promises success, rapid promotion and self assertion at all costs; it is an invitation to sexuality lived irresponsibly and a life devoid of interests and respect for others. Open your eyes wide, dear young people; this is not the way that leads to joy and to life, but the path that sinks into sin and death. Jesus says: "If any man would come after me, let him deny himself and take up his cross and follow me. For whoever would save his life will lose it, and whoever loses his life for my sake will find it" (Mt 16:24-25).

Jesus does not deceive us. With the truth of his words, which sound harsh but fill the heart with peace, he reveals to us the secret of authentic life. By accepting the condition and destiny of man, he overcame sin and death and, rising, transformed the Cross from a tree of death into a tree of life. He is God-with-us, Christ is God-with-us, Emmanuel (Mt 1:23), who came to share our whole life. He does not leave us alone on the cross. Jesus is the faithful love that does not abandon us and knows how to turn the night into the dawn of hope. If the Cross is accepted, it generates salvation and brings peace, as is evidenced by *the many beautiful testimonies given by young believers. Without God, the Cross crushes us; with God, it redeems and saves us. "Take up your Cross!" accept it, do not let yourself be crushed by events, but conquer evil and death with Christ! If you make the Gospel of the Cross your life project, if you follow Jesus all the way to the Cross, you will find yourself fulfilled!*

16. As I Have Loved You

When Jesus commanded us to love with perfect love, "as I have loved you," history was forever changed. JPII teaches us that the "as" of this "as I have loved you" shows us the degree of the love with which Jesus loves us. It is with this very fullness and perfection of love that we are called to love one another because we are destined for the richness and fullness of love. We learn somethin here, big time, about love: we learn with Jesus to practice the humility of renunciation. B16 reminded us on Christmas 2006 that this practice of the humility of renunciation belongs to the very essence of love. In *Veritatis Splendor* #20, while commentin on "as I have loved you," JPII says, "Jesus continues with words which indicate the sacrificial gift of his life on the Cross, as the witness to a love 'to the end' (Jn 13:1): 'Greater love has no man than this, that a man lay down his life for his friends' (Jn 15:13)."

---

*G*reat love can change small things into great ones.

Great love can change small things into great ones, and it is only love which lends value to our actions. And the purer our love becomes, the less there will be within us for the flames of suffering to feed on, and the suffering will cease to be suffering for us; it will become a delight! By the grace of God, I have received such a disposition of heart that I am never so happy as when I suffer for Jesus, whom I love with every beat of my heart.

— St. Faustina, *Notebook* #303

To learn somethin about love, about practicin the humility of renunciation, is to learn how to draw from the power of the victorious love of Jesus. We learn how to draw from the power of the victorious love of Jesus by gettin into the logic of service and humility, and also by lettin somethin of this logic get into us. On December 25, 2001, JPII pushed and challenged us by sayin, "It's up to us to draw from the power of his victorious love by appropriating his 'logic' of service and humility." This is also connected with the logic of sharin and solidarity which prepares us to make radical renouncements.

A radical lettin-go of self into the hands of Love.

A radical letting-go of our self is only possible if in the process we end up, not by falling into the void, but into the hands of Love eternal. Only the love of God, who loses himself for us and gives himself to us, makes it possible for us also to become free, to let go, and so truly to find life.

— B16, St. Stephen's Cathedral, Vienna, Sunday, September 9, 2007

Learnin how to make radical renouncements requires a radical lettin-go of ourselves. B16 helps us with this, in that he reminds us that it's only possible by fallin into the hands of Love. The freedom to fall into the hands of Love is a moment acquired by Love alone, and it's by contemplatin Christ Crucified that we can begin to understand the full meanin of freedom, the freedom that is necessary for and given for love by Love. It is in this freedom that we learn and accomplish the giving of our selves in communion with the never-endin source of Love, with the very love with which Jesus loved us.

Freedom is acquired in love and in the gift of self.

Jesus reveals by his whole life, and not only by his words, that freedom is acquired in love, that is, in the gift of self. The one who says: "Greater love has no man than this, that a man lay down his life for his friends" (Jn 15:13), freely goes out to meet his Passion (cf. Mt 26:46), and in obedience to the Father gives his life on the Cross for all men (cf. Phil 2:6-11). Contemplation of Jesus Crucified is thus the high road which the Church must tread every day if she wishes to understand the full meaning of freedom: the gift of self in service to God and one's brethren. Communion with the Crucified and Risen Lord is the never-ending source from which the Church draws unceasingly in order to live in freedom, to give of herself and to serve.

— JPII, VS #87

The logic of service and humility, the practice of the humility of renunciation and learnin how to make radical renouncements are all part of learnin how to love as Jesus has loved us. By discoverin Jesus in the Eucharist, we enter into the school of freedom and charity by which we learn to love; in this school we become empowered with the love that enables us to fulfill the commandment of love. As I said in my song (for complete lyrics, visit www.francescoproductions.com) "School of the Eucharist":

At this school when I sit even just a little bit
I get hit with the power that made the veil
*   in the temple split*
When I submit fall on the floor and adore
Can't get enough got to come back for some more
Every prostitute and sinner every fool and hypocrite
Can benefit in this school repent and commit

As the incense rises up in adoration of the throne
Somethin happens to my wounded heart from
   all the love revealed and shown
Bright light Shekinah comes to my aid to assist
To change and sustain the way I think and exist
To feel the bliss because my name is in
   the book of life's list
That's what happens when you sit at the school
   of the Eucharist

Discoverin Jesus in the school of the Eucharist, the school of freedom and charity, teaches us to learn big time about love and puttin that love into action through makin a more complete gift of ourselves like Jesus. JPII put it like this: "If you learn to discover Jesus in the Eucharist you will also know how to discover Him in your brothers and sisters, particularly in the very poor. The Eucharist received with Love and Adored with Fervor becomes a School of Freedom and Charity in order to fulfill the commandment to Love. Jesus speaks to us in the wonderful language of the gift of self and of love so great as to give our own life for it. Is this an easy thing? You know very well that it is *not*! It is not easy to forget oneself, but if we do it draws us away from possessive and narcissistic love and opens up to us the joy of a love that is self-giving. This Eucharistic School of Freedom and Charity teaches us to overcome superficial emotions in order to be rooted firmly in what is true and good. It frees us from self-attachment in order to open ourselves to others. It teaches us to make the transition from an affective (emotional) love to an effective (ready for service or action) love operative, for love is not merely a feeling; it is an act of will that consists of preferring, in a constant manor, the good of others to the good of oneself. 'Greater love has no man than this, that a man lays down his life for his friends (Jn 15:13)'" (Feb 22, 2004, #5, Message for Cologne World Youth Day).

17. If You Love Me

Jesus makes it plain and simple and plain and clear in John 14:15: "If you love me, you will keep my commandments." In other words the connection between love and obedience is vitally important. The really big lesson here to help us learn somethin about love is how Jesus defines love by virtue of the obedience we must strive to practice. If we love him, we keep the commandments — boom — that's it. We show our love by keepin the commandments. The opposite of this truth is also true; if we don't love him, we disobey his words and don't keep his commandments. Jesus said, "Whoever does not love me does not keep my words; and the word that you hear is not mine, but is from the Father who sent me" (Jn 14:24). Jesus radicalizes disobedience by revealin the communion of love between Him and the Father — there's double-trouble. In other words, when we don't keep the word of the Word of Love, we're not keepin the Word of the Father of Love either, and that's a whole lot of falterin and flounderin with love. Don't want to do that.

Amongst other things, Jesus is helpin us to avoid any ambiguous sentimentality which can darken the light of the truth of love, and subject us to the tendencies and inclinations of impoverished love. Erasmo sternly reminds us, "God is love, not all love is God, mere affection is not God; sentimentality is not God" (Erasmo, *Love's Sacred Order*, p. 47). Yet, at the same time, love burnin in our hearts will keep us in the light of truth so we can embrace the demands of love in the spirit and fact of obedience. This is how we can keep on strivin to persevere and prevent our hearts from growin cold as a result of the increase of evil.

I love how AJH flipped a famous philosophical line by Descartes. Descartes said, "I think, therefore I am." AJH, bein a radical lover of truth rooted in the depths of Jewish tradition and the best of Jewish mysticism said, "I am commanded, therefore I am." That says it all with regard to obedience. For von B, obedience increases our capacity for achievement by taken us into the supernatural. He uses the example of someone askin us to do somethin to which we reply, "I can't"; but if it's imposed on me in obedience, my capacity for achievin whatever is bein imposed on is lifted up, kinda-like supersized, enhanced with the lift of supernatural power.

Ultimately, it's like Jesus in the Garden of Gethsemane. The crushin reality of the Cross and immanent crucifixion seemed to be too much. This did not stop Jesus but energized and intensified his prayer, which kept him on the path of love; Jesus prayed to the Father for the unbearable dimensions of this cup of love to pass over him. Yet, in and through his prayer, obedience unleashed its torrential showers of love which lifted Jesus high on the Cross, which pierced him wide open to reveal for all access to the lavish and torrential dimensions of love.

Love links obedience with responsibility for the possibility of what JPII calls "the full obedience of love." This link not only keeps love real and rooted in the historical realities that make demands on our love, it also helps us grow and develop into the full enrichin mystery of love. JPII was down-under in Auckland, New Zealand, on November 22, 1986, and said, "If you want to attain the fullness of joy, your obedience must be the full obedience of love. We should not be surprised that all true love requires sacrifice.... Do not be afraid when love makes demands. Do not be afraid when love requires sacrifice."

One of the greatest and most radical postmodern examples and witnesses to this full obedience of love is Blessed Mother Teresa. She used to like to say, "Submission for someone who is in love is more than a duty, it is blessedness." This is somethin she paraphrased and made her own from Louis Collins: "Submission for someone who is in love is more than a duty; it is more than a necessity it is a taste of blessedness" (cf. Mother Teresa, *Come Be My Light*, p. 366, note 12). It has been revealed to the world through her personal writings how deep and dark her journey was into the full obedience of love. And it was this full obedience of love that kept her faithful and fruitful in spite of and along with all that she experienced; what she felt, what she didn't feel, with all that she suffered with the power of the full obedience of love.

The possibility of the free response of a full love.

And so we find revealed the authentic and original aspect of the commandment of love and of the perfection to which it is ordered: we are speaking of a possibility opened up to man exclusively by grace, by the gift of God, by his love. On the other hand, precisely the awareness of having received the gift, of possessing in Jesus Christ the love of God, generates and sustains the free response of a full love for God and the brethren, as the Apostle John insistently reminds us in his first Letter: "Beloved, let us love one another; for love is of God and knows God. He who does not love does not know God; for God is love.... Beloved, if God so loved us, we ought also to love one another.... We love, because he first loved us" (1 Jn 4:7-8, 11, 19). This inseparable connection between the Lord's grace and human freedom, between gift and task, has been expressed in simple yet profound words by Saint Augustine in his prayer: "Da quod iubes et iube quod vis" (grant what you command and command what you will). The gift does not lessen but reinforces the moral demands of love: "This is his commandment, that we should believe in the name of his Son Jesus Christ and love one another just as he has commanded us" (1 Jn 3:32). One can "abide" in love only by keeping the commandments, as Jesus states: "If you keep my commandments, you will abide in my love, just as I have kept my Father's commandments and abide in his love" (Jn 15:10).

— JPII, VS #24

18. Wound of Love

The theater of the coexistence of good and evil.

The history of mankind is the theatre of the coexistence of good and evil. So even if evil exists alongside good, good perseveres beside evil and grows from the same soil, namely human nature. This human nature has not become totally corrupt, despite original sin. Nature has retained its capacity for good, as history confirms.

— JPII, *Memory and Identity*

The dignity and destiny of the human person is rooted in and flows from the wound of love — the pierced side and heart of Jesus. As B16 said, our definition of love must begin from this point (cf. DCE #12). The mystery and destiny of the human person is rooted in love. Albacete challenges us that we must possess and be defined by the capacity we have to sustain our "freedom to love through co-suffering." This capacity that sustains our freedom to love through sufferin gives rise to a new mission, a mission which is rooted in the "new order of love." This new mission is joined to what Albacete creatively calls "the community of redemptive suffering which helps complete what may be lacking in its inner resources to offer a home to those who suffer, sparing them from the loneliness that is hell. In other words, love strengthens us to carry pain with love" (cf. Albacete, *God at the Ritz*, pp. 114-116). As JPII confirms, "Human suffering has reached its culmination in the passion of Christ. At the same time, it has entered into a completely new dimension and a new order: it has been linked to love" (JPII, *Salvifici Doloris* #18). The wound of love gives rise to this new order of love, which strengthens us to carry pain with love, helping others to know that they are definitively loved.

If you do a quick comparison/contrast with the word love you get somethin like this: love/hate — heaven/hell. Albacete sheds light on the darkness and complete loneliness of hell. B16 with his clear and precise description of hell in SS #45 shows us why: "With death, our life-choice becomes definitive — our life stands before the judge. Our choice, which in the course of an entire life takes on a certain shape, can have a variety of forms. There can be people who have totally destroyed their desire for truth and readiness to love, people for whom everything has become a lie, and people who have lived for hatred and have suppressed all love within themselves. This is a terrifying thought, but alarming profiles of this type can and the destruction of good would be irrevocable: this is what we mean by the word *Hell*" (cf. CCC 1033-1037).

KW/JPII assures us, "There is no need to be dismayed if love sometimes follows tortuous ways. Grace has the power to make straight the paths of human love" (*Love and Responsibility* #140). This is a truth that gets lived out by virtue of us plungin ever anew into the energies of the great transformation. The energies of the great transformation of love protect and prevent us from abidin in death by keeping us lovin. 1 John 3:14 reveals the ultimate consequence of not lovin: "We know that we have passed out of death into life, because we love the brethren. He who does not love abides in death." So, if we don't want to abide in death, we got 2 love. The wound of love sustains and enriches us in the midst of our failed and impoverished attempts to love. The wound of love keeps us goin in the right direction just as the wound of original sin never stops tryin to get us off the path of true love.

The wound of original sin continually creates a struggle for us to love. Even in light of the victory of love the struggle goes on in the human heart to fulfill the demands of love up to the end. However, the good news is that the love that goes to the end has prevailed and strengthens us to do the same. JPII reminds us, "Humankind, created for freedom, bears within itself the wound of original sin, which constantly draws persons toward evil and puts them in need of redemption. Through Christ's sacrifice on the cross, the victory of the kingdom of God has been achieved once and for all. Nevertheless, the Christian life involves a struggle against temptation and the forces of evil. Only at the end of history when the Lord returns in glory for the final judgment (cf Matt. 25:31) with the establishment of a new heaven and a new Earth (cf 2 Pet 3:13, Rev 21:1); but as long as time lasts the struggle between good and evil continues in the human heart itself" (JPII, CA #25).

In light of all this, it's crucial for us to keep in mind that the wound of love is greater than the wound of original sin. B16 attested to this truth on September 8, 2007, in Austria at the Shrine of Mariazell: "God can write straight even on the crooked lines of our history. God allows us our freedom, and yet in our failures he can always find new paths for his love." The wound of love that wounds to heal unleashes the new order of love through sufferin. This new order of love gives rise to fruitful lovers who exercise their capacity to carry pain in the midst of a culture that has become so impoverished that these lovers seem to become extinct. Yet, at the same time, there is a new army of radical, rebellious, reckless warriors of love risin up. These postmodern love warriors, like St. Thomas the Apostle, take the plunge into the Love wounds of the crucified, resurrected, and glorified body of Jesus and are thus rendered unstoppable with the love that is stronger than death.

The digital domain of postmodern culture that was born to exalt the human person winds up impoverishin and destroyin the human person instead. "Generation digital" has become so wounded by the destructive energies of impoverished love that this wound can give the impression that there is no prospect or hope for healin. Events give rise to a false and accelerated sense of intimacy through technology that become completely internalized. This false and deceptive internalization of events creates the illusion that we don't need to be healed because we think, and wrongly at that, that we're so well connected that all is well. The illusion of becomin closer becomes more real, and the disappointment of really not bein so connected becomes more intense; many or most cases remain undetected, resultin in greater disappointment and unhappiness. This deception of an accelerated and false intimacy becomes a tyrannical power deprivin us of our experience and identity as persons created and destined to be infinitely and definitively loved.

R adical, rebellious warriors of reckless love need to break the tyranny of conformity.

Tyranny as an oppressive power creates a tyranny of conformity which needs to be exposed and overcome by radical, rebellious warriors of reckless love. Our inner identity as persons infinitely and definitively love needs to be brought to the mainstream culture with the power of truth and responsibility for the cause of love. AJH puts it like this:

The tyranny of conformity tends to deprive man of his inner identity, of his ability to stand still in the midst of flux, to remain a person in the midst of a crowd. Thus the threat to modern man is loss of personhood, vanishing of identity, sinking into anonymity, not knowing who he is, whence he comes, and where he goes.

— AJH, *Moral Grandeur and Spiritual Audacity*, p. 32

The spirit of love showers riches upon us to be shared.

If we recognize ourselves as poor in the presence of God, this being the truth, and not a false humility — we will have the heart of one who is poor, the eyes and hands of the poor, in order to share the riches which God has lavished upon us.... The spirit of love showers upon us a thousand good things to be shared; the more we seek them, the more we shall receive them in abundance.

— JPII, Lent 1987

19. Destined to Love

In order for us to have a clear sense, a burnin passion, for the reality and fact that we are destined to love requires help from a "supernatural perspective." This supernatural perspective is required in order for us to have a fruitful understandin of the task entrusted to us as persons. B16 described this supernatural perspective as bein rooted in the dignity of the human person created in the image and likeness of God who is Love. In his message for World Day of Peace on January 1, 2007, B16 describes this supernatural perspective as bein rooted in the ability of each person for "self knowledge" and "free self-giving" and "entering into communion with others." It is from this "supernatural perspective that one can understand the task entrusted to human beings: to mature in the ability to love and to contribute to the progress of the world renewing it in justice and peace."

To mature in the ability to love.

"Self knowledge" and "free self-giving" and "entering into communion with others." It is from this supernatural perspective, that one can understand the task entrusted to human beings: to mature in the ability to love and to contribute to the progress of the world renewing it in justice and peace.

— B16, World Day of Peace, January 1, 2007

We are destined to love because we were created by Love for love. God, who is Love, has put love in us from the beginnin. It's very much who we are as creatures created in the image and likeness of God who is Love. Once again, love is a power which enables us to participate in the love with which

God loves us so we can experience the love that surpasses our bein in control of it so that love can become greater and stronger. This is the "surpassing knowledge" St. Paul talks about in Ephesians 3:19. To surpass means to become better, greater, or stronger than usual, to go beyond. We can transcend a fear-based and impoverished love and transform it by movin into the realm of Ephesians 3:19 so that we may be "filled to the measure of the fullness of God;" in other words into the full measure of love.

From Love comes the vocation of all to communion.

From God being communion derives the vocation of all humanity.

— JPII, Angelus, Trinity Sunday 2003

Because we are destined to love, love is the superabundant answer to all questions about the meanin and purpose of our lives. The Church teaches in CCC 68: "By love, God has revealed himself and given himself to man. He has provided the definitive superabundant answer to the questions that man asks himself about the meaning and purpose of his life." Our destiny to love becomes distracted by the many levels of deception at work in the culture and at work in our lives. On March 7, 1985, JPII made the connection of deception and the deprivation of human destiny: "Deception is a deprivation of human dignity and a distraction from human destiny.... It has its origins in the father of lies. God, on the other hand, is the author of truth. And it is the right and the responsibility of the Church to be not only the communicator of truth but its defender."

Our dignity is rooted in love.

The freedom which comes from truth can give the human family a vision of what it can be, of what it should be — and it can give to every human being awareness of the destiny God has prepared for us because of the dignity he has conferred upon us.... He has called us into being because of love, and he sustains us in being because of love.

— JPII, March 7, 1985

Those of us who are incorporated into the Church as persons destined to love are not guaranteed our salvation; it does not negate us from perseverin in practicing love. That's why CCC 837 incorporates *Lumen Gentium* (LG) 14 as she gives us the followin bold warnin: "Even though incorporated into the Church, one who does not however persevere in charity is not saved. He remains indeed in the bosom of the Church, but 'in body' not 'in heart'" (LG 14). We cannot live without love because we are destined to love. We remain incomplete and unfulfilled if we do not experience love. We are destined to be happy, and the ultimate enrichment of humanity and human love comes through the knowledge and experience of bein infinitely and definitively loved. "Happy is the person of love who has caused God, who is love, to dwell in his heart" (Bishop Martyrius, late seventh century in Beth Garmai, near Kirkuk, Iraq, *Magnificat*, Vol. 8, No. 9, November 2006, p. 31).

Freedom comes from bein made capable to enter into the mystery of love.

Today there is an urgent need to recover the vision of an organic unity embracing man and all of human history.

Christians are convinced that at the heart of this unity is the mystery of Christ, the Incarnate Word of God, who reveals man to himself and discloses his sublime vocation (cf. Gaudium et Spes, 22). Do not be afraid of Christ! Faith in him opens before us a spiritual world that has inspired and continues to inspire humanity's intellectual and artistic energies. Christ sets us free for authentic creativity precisely because he makes us capable of entering into the mystery of Love, the love of God and the love of man, and in doing so he makes it possible for us to appreciate and at the same time to transcend particularity.... Where such a vision is weak, human dignity is diminished, and the goods of creation, meant for the benefit and progress of humanity, sooner or later turn against man and against life. The century now drawing to a close, with its painful experiences of war, violence, torture and various forms of ideological oppression, testifies all too eloquently to this. At the same time, it stands as a witness to the enduring power of the human spirit to triumph over all that seeks to suffocate the irrepressible quest for truth and freedom.

— JPII, September 11, 1999

As some of you may know, family to me is an acronym — Forget About Me I Love You. To forget about oneself while maintainin and becomin one's best self requires purification. Purification is a vital dimension of the work of Love. The purpose of the purifyin energies of love is to yield an ever-expandin increase of love so we can be more love and do more love and fulfill our destiny. This movement is necessary regardless of who we are or what we may be able to do and accomplish, because if we have not love, "we are nothing" (1 Cor 13:2). This capacity for bein and doin more love flows from the liberatin force of the Gospel of Jesus, which purifies us — heart, mind, body, and soul — with the fire of the Love that is God. As the Church teaches in CCC 2519, "Purity of heart is the precondition of the vision of God. Even now it enables us to see *according to* God, to accept others as 'neighbors'; it lets us perceive the human body — ours and our neighbor's — as the temple of the Holy Spirit, a manifestation of divine beauty."

R eflectin on destiny reveals the inner logic of love.

Knowledge of the natural moral norm is not inaccessible to those who, in reflecting on themselves and their destiny, strive to understand the inner logic of the deepest inclinations present in their being. Albeit not without hesitation and doubt, they are capable of discovering, at least in its essential lines, this common moral law which, over and above cultural differences, enables human beings to come to a common understanding regarding the most important aspects of good and evil, justice and injustice. It is essential to go back to this fundamental law, committing our finest intellectual energies to this quest, and not letting ourselves be discouraged by mistakes and misunderstandings.... Mankind is not "lawless."... The growth of a global juridic culture depends, for that matter, on a constant commitment to strengthen the profound human content of international norms, lest they be reduced to mere procedures, easily subject to manipulation for selfish or ideological reasons.

— B16, Message for World Peace, January 1, 2008

20. One Flesh

For the impoverishment of love to be enriched, liberated, and able to participate in the ever-expandin full grandeur of love, it needs to be healed. The oneness, the unity and fullness of humanity and the fullness of divinity in the flesh of the Word made flesh is the ultimate reality of this unity. As Antonio Prieto gratefully asserts, "Thanks to the 'logos,' in effect, body and sexuality may be integrated into the totality of our existential freedom, so that love may be transformed into the living expression of our whole being and not remain a purely biological phenomenon" (*The Way of Love*, pp. 214-215).

A deep bond which transcends the impulse of youth.

The love of a man and a woman is based on a deep bond which transcends the impulse of youth. This love is welded together by something "else," which objectifies itself in the form of a baby, a child, or, to express it more generically, a task. And when there is this child, then what is the task? It is either consciously or obscurely, nebulously, the destiny of the child, his journey as a human person. It is this sense that brings forth and dictates the attitude of real emotion in the parents, a firm commitment, a loving feeling in all of its simplicity and totality. Without this something else which exceeds the relationship, the relationship would not last. A relationship needs a reason, and the true reason for a relationship must tie it to the whole.

— Giussani, *The Religious Sense*, pp. 61-62

The impoverishment of love tragically reduces the body and sexuality to what JPII refers to as "pure materiality," "simply a complex of organs, functions, and energies to be used according to the sole criteria of pleasure and efficiency." The sacrament of Matrimony (Marriage) has the potential, as well as the cultural necessity and responsibility of renewin and reestablishin the awesomeness of the reality and mystery of "one flesh" in the midst of the depersonalization and exploitation of sexuality. The body, as JPII said, "is no longer perceived as a properly personal reality, a sign and place of relations with others, with God and with the world" (EV #23).

A love which renounces itself in favor of the other.

Eros, this gift of love between a man and a woman, comes from the same source of the goodness of the Creator, as does the possibility of a love, which renounces the self in favor of the other. Self-sacrificial love can transform erotic love so that one no longer seeks his own joy and pleasure, but seeks first of all the good of the other person.

— B16, January 18, 2006, General Audience

When we no longer see, or worse still if we never see the body as the expression of the language of love, the result will be another explosion of self-hatred. B16 in DCE #5 specifically mentions "hatred of bodiliness" which is deeply connected to and flows from the toxic cultural waste of the consumer culture. It's tragically energized by the media culture and the "cash is king" fallacy. Christopher West makes a really honest point about these toxic cultural tactics: "For every bodily flaw the media brainwashes us into believing we have, that same media will sell us some products or procedure to correct it. From breast implants to hair transplants, from exotic skin creams to stranger-than-fiction exercise machines, from buttocks reduction by liposuction to abs of steel for sex appeal: these are the new 'sacraments' and 'liturgical rituals' for a false cult of the body" (*The Love That Satisfies*, p. 56). Real true, enrichin and lastin happiness is rooted in love, and the mystery of original innocence releases what JPII calls "a beautifying immunity from shame as the result of love" (JPII, Jan. 30, 1980). We got 2 love because we got 2 be energetically and truthfully engaged in the mission of restorin beauty to the life of culture. This "beautifyin" as the result of love will help bring about healin from the impoverishin defects caused by shame with the irreversible and infinite love of the Father.

The beautifyin immunity from shame as the result of love.

Happiness is being rooted in love. Original happiness speaks to us of the beginning of man, who emerged from love and initiated love. That happened in an irrevocable way, despite the subsequent sin and death. In his time, Christ will be a witness to this irreversible love of the Creator and Father, which had already been expressed in the mystery of creation and in the grace of original innocence. The common beginning of man and woman, that is, the original truth of their body in masculinity and femininity, to which Genesis 2:25 draws our attention, does not know shame. This beginning can also be defined as the original and beautifying immunity from shame as the result of love. This immunity directs us toward the mystery of man's original innocence. It is a mystery of his existence, prior to the knowledge of good and evil and almost "outside" it.

— JPII, January 30, 1980

B16 on May 2, 2007, gave a teachin on one of the great early Church Fathers, Origen. Origen was convinced that the best way to become acquainted with God is through love: "There is no authentic scientia Christi without falling in love with him.... According to Origen the highest degree of knowledge of God stems from love." What's good for the goose is good for the gander; the same thing applies to human beings: "Only if there is love, if hearts are opened, can one person truly know the other.... The Hebrew verb to know ... is used to express the human act of love: 'Adam knew his wife Eve, and she conceived' (Gen 4:1). This suggests that the union in love procures the most authentic knowledge. Just as the man and the woman are 'two in one flesh,' so God and the believer become 'two in one spirit.'" The whole "one flesh thing" is broken open into the realm of our relationship with God to the point where it's possible for God and us to become "two in one spirit." This kind of relationship based on love will have demands; the demands of love are many and constant.

These demands of love are crucial for every relationship, and they are beautiful, especially for man and woman united in marriage. On May 28, 1986, JPII reminded us that it's "necessary to offer the beauty and attraction of God's plan for marriage and the family in order to strengthen the will of today's men and women to live up to the greatness of this plan, while being aware of the demands it involves." These demands of love are met with the energy of love flowin from the heart of God into the hearts of men and women which in turn becomes the energy that renews the world and the cultures therein. Check out B16 on November 4, 2007: "Love, flowing from the heart of God and working through the heart of man, is the force that renews the world."

This union of one flesh and one spirit with love heals the gap that prevents the union and communion of love takin root in the lives of real people in the midst of the real challenges and obstacles in their respective cultures. As Christopher West would say, holiness is not loved. But when holiness is loved and the degree that holiness is loved, the healin takes place: "Each time a human heart receives and reciprocates God's love, true reconciliation of divinity and humanity, body and soul, man and woman takes root" (*The Theology of the Body Explained*, Pauline Books and Media, 2003, p. 28). The specific area of the divorce culture which gives rise to a divorce mentality stands in the midst of a really intense need for this gap between flesh and spirit, love and holiness to be healed. Accordin to West, "A divorce-mentality results from a counterfeit love that never reaches the great dignity and unrepeatability of the person, but only values those diminishable and repeatable attributes that bring self-gratification" (ibid., p. 163).

We need more than ever men and women deeply convicted of the demands of love with a "u got 2 love" mentality in order to unleash revolutionary energies of love in the heart of the battle of love in the heart of the world. We need men and women united in love to become couples who are radical revolutionary warriors of reckless love; men and women who know themselves to be infinitely and definitively loved and who will then likewise be able to love each other with the very love with which they are loved.

This will help all the challenges, stress, and tensions of married life and the flesh become what Erasmo calls "dynamized" as a result of the explosion of love in the heart of the "great mystery" of the Passion and Resurrection of Jesus. Openness to, dependence on, and communion with this lover will cause a transformation generated and sustained by the energy of the love of Jesus. As Erasmo rightly asserts, all this can be transformed by Christ's love, "so that the use of the passions and the energies of the body and soul become revolutionary" (Erasmo, *Love's Sacred Order*, p. 53).

21. Crucified Love

The supreme triumph of self-abandoned charity.

Having roused the hostility of official religion by His generous freedom of Love, He was condemned by a combination of political cowardice and ecclesiastical malice to a barbarous and degrading death; and made of that death the supreme triumph of self-abandoned charity.

— Evelyn Underhill, *The School of Charity*, p. 52

The most amazin thing about Crucified Love is that once we embrace it, it opens us up to the mysterious purposes of Love. The reality of love and life through the energy of Crucified Love protects us from separatin the different dimensions of love, which is the root cause of the impoverishment of love. Crucified Love is the ultimate source of the enrichment of love and activates our capacity for makin a gift of ourselves to the mysterious purposes of Love. It presses us to embrace the whole of life and love, and not just some reduced "spiritual" dimension of it. It's the intense fire of love that burns on the altar of our hearts: "Your heart is the altar of God. It is here that the fire of intense love must always burn. You are to feed it every day with the wood of the Cross of Christ and commemoration of his Passion" (St. Bonaventure, *The Perfection of Life*).

Self-given to the mysterious purposes of charity.

The Light of the World enters our life to show us reality; and forces us to accept the fact that it is the whole of that life,

not some supposed spiritual part of it, which is involved in our
response to God, and must be self-given to the mysterious
purposes of charity.

— Evelyn Underhill, *School of Charity*, p. 52

B16 in DCE precisely locates the startin point and method for us to attempt to understand and to stand under the reality and power of Crucified Love: *contemplating the pierced side of Christ*. He makes a definitive conclusion about such definitive love: "It is from there (the pierced side of Christ) that our definition of love must begin" (DCE #12). When the pierced side of Christ is not the point of reference for our learnin somethin about love, we will not be able to stand under and be carried by the torrent of Crucified Love. It's only by, as B16 said, "looking at Jesus dead on the Cross for us" that the truth God is love can be known and contemplated. It's in this contemplation of Christ Crucified that we discover the path along which our life and love must move. This torrential love gushin forth from the pierced side of Christ Crucified is the source of the love that God — Who is Love — lavishes upon us. B16 revealed this as his intention in DCE #1: "I wish in my first Encyclical to speak of the love which God lavishes upon us and which we in turn must share with others." This lavishin of so great a love triggers an awareness that evokes a response from within us to live from the flow of this torrential love.

However, there's a bit of an obstacle. So often awareness of our weaknesses and limitations, or the painful reminder of our weaknesses and limitations by others, all of which flow from the toxic waste of impoverished love, impels us to run away and take refuge in lesser forms of love. At the end of the day, it's only the extreme humility of Crucified Love that can sweep us away with overflowin grace — the overflowin richness of the Love which makes us know ourselves as definitively and infinitely loved.

A deep sense of our limitations with the certainty of Christ's enduring love.

Before Christ crucified we remember that, in contrast to the overflowing grace which makes the Church "holy," we her children are deeply marked by sin, and cast a shadow upon the face of the Bride of Christ: no self-exultation therefore but a deep sense of our limitations and weaknesses. Yet we cannot but be filled with joy, with that inner joy to which the Prophets call us, a joy rich in thanksgiving and praise, because it is based on our awareness of the gifts received and our certainty of Christ's enduring love.

— JPII, January 6, 2001

Crucified love is extreme love to the extremist degree. Crucified love reverses the impoverishin effects of impoverished love and enables those who embrace the Cross to embark on the journey into the embrace of the very fullness of Love. In this embrace of Christ's enduring love, we receive the fullness of love we need and are destined for, the ultimate and absolute love that provides for our needs and carries us along every second and minute of every hour each day; the love that gives meaning and value to our sufferin and the sufferin of all who suffer. This gift of love must be received and welcomed. B16 reminds us that we cannot always give love, we must receive love as a gift (cf. DCE #7); we can't give what we don't have. JPII made the same point regardin us bein made capable of love only by receivin love as a gift.

Love received makes us capable of love.

We become capable of love only by a gift received.

— JPII, *The Splendor of the Truth* #22

The reception of the gift of Ultimate and Absolute Love in the embrace of Crucified Love enables us to become a source from which rivers of livin water flow: "He who believes in me, as the scripture has said, 'Out of is heart shall flow rivers of living water'" (Jn 7:38). B16 tells us "to become such a source, one must constantly drink anew from the original source, which is Jesus Christ, from whose pierced heart flows the love of God" (DCE #7). We can live from the stream of this love. This pierced heart of the Crucified takes us into a new dimension of love — the new order of love. Here human sufferin reaches a place where we can experience meaning and value in our sufferin because of Crucified Love: "Human suffering has reached its culmination in the passion of Christ. At the same time, it has entered into a completely new dimension and a new order: it has been linked to love" (JP, *Salvifici Doloris* #18).

The solution of all difficulties.

The solution of all difficulties is Christ, and Christ crucified.

— Blessed John XXIII

Crucified love can be seen in a picture created by the life and example of Fr. Walter Ciszek who died in 1984. He was in the Soviet prison system for twenty-three years durin World War II convicted as a spy for the Vatican. He wrote about takin up the Cross every day — this is how we enter into the embrace of Crucified Love. It's not easy. It will involve bein exhausted, dealin with the unspectacular dimensions of daily routine with its difficulties and pain, puttin aside our pleasures and happiness, the people and things we really want until another time, so we can be present to what's really needed at the moment: "taking up daily the same Cross of Christ.... It means getting up each morning and going to bed exhausted. It means the routine, not the spectacular. It can mean drudgery, pain, putting aside pleasures, happiness, or the love the human heart craves until another time, so that what is necessary at the moment can be done."

₱aily work and the mystery of the Cross.

Daily work ... draws a person closer to the mystery of the Cross: it is a redemptive activity; it is a necessity and a liberation.

— JPII, March 18, 1991

Mad Eros.

On the Cross, God's eros for us is made manifest. Eros is indeed — as Pseudo Dionysius expresses it — that force "that does not allow the lover to remain in himself but moves him to become one with the beloved" (De divinis nominibus, IV, 13: PG 3, 712). Is there more "mad eros" (N. Cabasilas, Vita in Cristo, 648) than that which led the Son of God to make Himself one with us even to the point of suffering as His own the consequences of our offenses?

— B16, Lent 2007

The Church teaches in CCC 1505 that, "On the cross Christ took upon himself the whole weight of evil." This takin on of the full weight of evil by Jesus on the Cross is what unleashes the opposite of the full weight of evil; the fullness of the richness of love — Crucified Love. JPII said that, "Precisely by means of his Cross Jesus must strike at the roots of evil planted in the history of man and in human souls" (JP, *Salvifici Doloris*, Feb 11, 1984). This root of evil planted in history is the source of all and every manifestation of impoverished love. It is precisely with this "strike" of the Crucified at the roots of evil in the world and in our souls that love is rooted and planted. With Christ dwellin in our hearts through faith we become "rooted and grounded in love" (Eph 3:17). Thus, bein rooted and grounded in Crucified Love, we have the possibility to unleash the creative power of Crucified Love "to comprehend with all the saints what is the breadth and length and height and depth, and to know the love of Christ which surpasses knowledge." This will embark us on a journey that we "may be filled with all the fullness of God" (Eph. 3:18-19).

This fullness of Crucified Love is a love that suffers, a love that is pure gift, a love that cannot be earned, a love that is not deserved. The truth of a love that suffers is affirmed beautifully by AJH (*Between God and Man*, ed. Rothschild, p.120): "A religion without man is as impossible as a religion without God. That God takes man seriously is shown by his concern for human existence. It finds its deepest expression in the fact that God can actually suffer. At the heart of the prophetic affirmation is the certainty that God is concerned about the world to the point of suffering." This love that suffers is no doubt a painful ordeal, and it also a love that gives joy.

The agony of the Cross and the truth God is love.

If the agony on the Cross had not happened, the truth that God is love would be unfounded.

— JPII, CTH, p. 66

TV culture tells us that "everybody loves Raymond." People like to look and laugh at scenarios on that popular show (*Everybody Loves Raymond*) through presentations of ordinary people strugglin to love and to be happy. This is true because everybody wants to be happy and everybody wants everybody to love them. How about we produce a show "Raymond Loves Everybody"? Wantin to be happy is a good thing. Bein happy is a better thing; but wantin to be happy without embracing sufferin ain't gonna happen without losin ourselves. This comin out of ourselves is a painful process and a necessary process if we are to mature — to grow up — and be happy and attain true joy. This is only gonna happen 4 real on the path of Crucified Love.

J oy develops only on the path of love which involves the Cross.

Love gives joy. But it is always a process of losing oneself, hence, a process of thinkin out of oneself; in this regard it is also a painful process. Only in this way is it beautiful and helps us to mature and to attain true joy. This joy however only develops on the path of love, and this path of love has to do with the Cross, with communion with the Crucified Christ.

— B16, March 2, 2007

Durin the canonization of a great Polish woman, Hedwiga, on June 8, 1997, JPII prayed to her: "Often you would kneel at the feet of the Crucified One at Wawel (the great Cathedral in Krakow) to learn this generous love from Christ, and learn it you did. You showed by your life that the greatest thing is love." Proof of our learnin somethin about love is to show through our life that love is the greatest thing. Learnin this generous love is a lifelong task and the work of conversion. On October 6, 1999, the great JPII said, "Conversion is aimed at fulfilling the commandment of Love.... The human person is called to Love God with total commitment and to relate to his brothers and sisters with a loving attitude inspired by God's own Love. Conversion means being converted to love."

Christ Crucified reveals to us the definitive reality of love and divine mercy — the secret of happiness. Learnin this generous love requires us to lose ourselves and to give ourselves which in turn requires us to drop the question "What do I get out of it?" Becomin less concerned with "What's in it for me?" will help us increase our trust in Love's power to provide. Love will conquer our fear of bein loved and of lovin, which will in turn secure our happiness.

---

*C*onversion means to depend on love.

Conversion consists in freely and lovingly accepting to depend in all things on God ... to depend on love.... Those who let themselves be conquered by him do not fear losing their life, for on the Cross he loved us and gave himself for us. It is precisely by losing our life for love that we discover it ... the Cross is the definitive revelation of love and divine mercy for us as well, men and women of this epoch, all too often distracted by earthly and transient apprehensions and concerns. God is love, and his love is the secret of our happiness. So it is that there is no other way to enter into this mystery of love than to lose ourselves, to give ourselves; the way of the Cross.

— B16, Ash Wednesday, February 21, 2007

---

22. Mother of Love

Mary helps the soul expand to be ready for the tasks of Love.

As soon as she perceives in any soul even the smallest similarity to her own ascent, she slips in and helps that soul expand so that it will be ready for the Son's tasks.... The Son works the actual transformation, but the mother helps to remove the difficulties that the person could have in comprehending the Son. Everything she does is done only according to the mind of the Son.

— Adrienne von Speyr, *Handmaid of the Lord*

Mary, the Mother of Love, reveals to us and gives to us the highest dimensions of our vocation to love — the fullness of Love, her Son Jesus. She helps us in a unique way to be equipped and ready for the tasks of her Son, most especially by standin at the foot of the Cross. As only a Mother can, Mary helps us to respond and embrace the perpetual need for us to go beyond ourselves in makin a more complete gift of ourselves. Mary, as the Mother of Love, helps our hearts to expand. To love means to expand. More precisely, as JPII put it, to love means to be a gift, to be filled with a generosity that makes us be for all, to be for each person with a generous heart, with generous love. As Adrienne put it, "Mary includes all and lets an eternal cycle of love between herself and her divine Son become living for everyone. She contributes to this vitality" (von Speyr, *Handmaid of the Lord*). The ultimate place where new love expands and Mary's new motherhood unleashes its universal mission of redemptive love is the foot of the Cross with the beloved disciple.

God the Father entrusted Mary with the love of motherhood.

Mary's motherhood, completely pervaded by her spousal attitude as the "handmaid of the Lord," constitutes the first and fundamental dimension of that mediation which the Church confesses and proclaims in her regard and continually "commends to the hearts of the faithful," since the Church has great trust in her. For it must be recognized that before anyone else it was God himself, the Eternal Father, who entrusted himself to the Virgin of Nazareth, giving her his own Son in the mystery of the Incarnation. Her election to the supreme office and dignity of Mother of the Son of God refers, on the ontological level, to the very reality of the union of the two natures in the person of the Word (hypostatic union). This basic fact of being the Mother of the Son of God is from the very beginning a complete openness to the person of Christ, to his whole work, to his whole mission. The words "Behold, I am the handmaid of the Lord" testify to Mary's openness of spirit: she perfectly unites in herself the love proper to virginity and the love characteristic of motherhood, which are joined and, as it were, fused together.

— JPII, *Mother of the Redeemer* #39

The generous heart.

Mary caused the heart of Jesus to reveal his generosity.... This is the generous heart, because fullness abides in it: in Christ, the true man, lives the fullness of divinity, and God is love. He is generous because he loves, and to love means to expand, to give. To love means to be a gift, it means to be for others, to be for all, to be for each person.

— JPII Angelus, August 3, 1986

New love — new motherhood at the foot of the Cross.

Undoubtedly, we find here an expression of the Son's particular solicitude for his Mother, whom he is leaving in such great sorrow. And yet the "testament of Christ's Cross" says more. Jesus highlights a new relationship between Mother and Son, the whole truth and reality of which he solemnly confirms. One can say that if Mary's motherhood of the human race had already been outlined, now it is clearly stated and established. It emerges from the definitive accomplishment of the Redeemer's Paschal Mystery. The Mother of Christ, who stands at the very center of this mystery — a mystery which embraces each individual and all humanity — is given as mother to every single individual and all mankind. The man at the foot of the Cross is John, "the disciple whom he loved." But it is not he alone. Following tradition, the Council does not hesitate to call Mary "the Mother of Christ and mother of mankind": since she "belongs to the offspring of Adam she is one with all human beings.... Indeed she is 'clearly the mother of the members of Christ ... since she cooperated out of love so that there might be born in the Church the faithful.'" And so this "new motherhood of Mary," generated by faith, is the fruit of the "new" love which came to definitive maturity in her at the foot of the Cross, through her sharing in the redemptive love of her Son.

— JPII, RM #23

Once our hearts have tasted the sweetness of havin been enlarged with a passion for generous service, we realize that a pure and generous love is the best witness to the reality of love; driven by a passionate pursuit of makin an ever-more generous gift of ourselves for the sake of others, for the sake of Love. Mary can help us to know "when it is time to speak of God and when it is better to say nothing and to let love alone speak." As the Mother of Love, Mary can help us like no one else to know by experience "that God is love (1 Jn 4:8) and that God's presence is felt at the very time when the only thing we do is to love" (B16, DCE #31).

For love to grow and develop in kind and degree, entrustment is necessary. This is the *totus tuus* (it's all yours) of the great JPII to Mary, Mother of the Redeemer, Mother of Love. In his encyclical *Mother of the Redeemer*, he refers to this entrustment: "such entrusting is the response to a person's love, and in particular to the love of a mother" (#45). Durin an Angelus message on August 15, 2002, JPII demonstrated the depth of his trust in and love for Mary: "With your help we do not fear obstacles and difficulties. Fatigue and sufferings do not discourage us because you accompany us on the path of life from heaven; you watch over all your children and fill them with grace. To you we entrust the destiny of peoples and the mission of the Church."

With great emotion JPII wrote on a piece of paper "*Totus tuus*."

Cardinal Dziwisz shares a very intimate and powerful moment which expresses the great love JPII had for and great ultimate trust and confidence he had in Mary, Mother of Love. Durin his last stays in the hospital with complications arisin due to the flu makin it extremely difficult and painful for JPII to breathe, a tracheotomy was required:

As soon as he revived from the anesthesia, with great emotion he wrote "Totus tuus" on a piece of paper, abandoning his whole life once again to Mary (Let Me Go to the Father's House, p. 32).

We see no greater manifestation of JPII's love and trust in the lovin and all powerful protection of Mary Mother of

Love, specifically as Our Lady of Fatima, than what we see when JPII speaks about the failed assassination attempt of May 13, 1981:

> *Again I have become indebted to the Blessed Virgin and to all the Patron saints. Could I forget that event in St. Peter's Square took place on the day and at the hour when the first appearance of the Mother of Christ to the poor little peasants has been remembered for over sixty years at Fatima in Portugal? For everything that happened to me on that very day, I felt that extraordinary motherly protection and care which turned out to be stronger than the deadly bullet.* (October 12, 1981, General Audience)

The Rosary mystically takes us to Mary's side until Christ is fully formed in us.

The Rosary mystically transports us to Mary's side as she is busy watching over the human growth of Christ in the home of Nazareth. This enables her to train us and to hold us with the same care, until Christ is "fully formed" in us (cf. Gal 4:19). This role of Mary, totally grounded in that of Christ and radically subordinated to it "in no way obscures or diminishes the unique mediation of Christ, but rather shows its power" (LG #60). This is the luminous principle expressed by the second Vatican council which I have so powerfully experienced in my own life and have made the basis of my Episcopal motto: "Totus tuus."

— JPII, *Apostolic Letter on the Rosary* #15

Mary, the Mother of Love can help us to conquer fear of intimacy and develop an authentic and appropriate sense of intimacy in all our relationships. This is a dimension of the sweetness of love. B16 in his 2007 message for Lent calls Mary *Mother of Beautiful Love.* Intimacy is a dimension of this beautiful love, and conversion to the love of Christ assures the authenticity of the growth and development of intimacy. So that's why B16 sees Mary as one who can help us grow ever deeper into *authentic conversion to the love of Christ*. The more we love Jesus, the more we will love Mary; the more we love Mary, the greater will be our heart's capacity to expand and embrace the people and events that are connected to the mysterious communion of Crucified Love. She helps us to live in intimacy with the mystery of her Son and the mysterious designs of the purposes of love from the depths of her heart, that requires from us an ever greater trust. As JPII said, by gazin upon Mary with love and trust in communion with her Son Jesus, "in her we see the world renewed in love" (EE #62).

Mary helps us live in intimacy with the mystery of love.

The Mother of that Son, therefore, mindful of what has been told her at the Annunciation and in subsequent events, bears within herself the radical "newness of faith": the beginning of the New Covenant. This is the beginning of the Gospel, the joyful Good News. However, it is not difficult to see in that beginning a particular heaviness of heart, linked with a sort of "night of faith" — to use the words of St. John of the Cross — a kind of "veil" through which one has to draw near to the Invisible One and to live in intimacy with the mystery. And this is the way that Mary, for many years, lived in intimacy with the mystery of her Son, and went forward in her "pilgrimage of faith," while Jesus "increased in wisdom ... and in favor with God and man" (Lk 2:52). God's predilection for him was manifested ever more clearly to people's eyes. The first human creature thus permitted to discover Christ was Mary, who lived with Joseph in the same house at Nazareth.

— JPII, *Mother of the Redeemer* #17

Mary shows us what love is and the constantly renewed power of love.

Mary has truly become the Mother of all believers. Men and women of every time and place have recourse to her motherly kindness and her virginal purity and grace, in all their needs and aspirations, their joys and sorrows, their moments of loneliness and their common endeavors. They constantly experience the gift of her goodness and the unfailing love which she pours out from the depths of her heart. The testimonials of gratitude, offered to her from every continent and culture, are a recognition of that pure love which is not self-seeking but simply benevolent. At the same time, the devotion of the faithful shows an infallible intuition of how such love is possible: it becomes so as a result of the most intimate union with God, through which the soul is totally pervaded by him — a condition which enables those who have drunk from the fountain of God's love to become in their turn a fountain from which "flow rivers of living water" (Jn 7:38). Mary, Virgin and Mother, shows us what love is and whence it draws its origin and its constantly renewed power. To her we entrust the Church and her mission in the service of love:

Holy Mary, Mother of God, you have given the world its true light, Jesus, your Son — the Son of God. You abandoned yourself completely to God's call and thus became a well spring of the goodness which flows forth from him. Show us Jesus. Lead us to him. Teach us to know and love him, so that we too can become capable of true love and be fountains of living water in the midst of a thirsting world.

— B16, DCE #42

The eyes of the dying JPII on Mary.

The eyes of the dying pope ... rested on an image of Our Lady of Czestochowa.

— Cardinal Dziwisz, *Let Me Go*, p. 38

23. Communion of Love

Love transforms the lover into the beloved.

The power of love is great and wonderful. Love perforce makes one to become like to that which one loves and like to that which one attains by love. There is nothing in life which unites and cements so firmly as love. It unites one to the beloved, and more, it transforms the lover into the beloved one. Love is naught else than a mutual and uniting strength.

— Diego de Estella (16th Century Franciscan Friar), *Meditations on the Love of God*, 1939, Sheed and Ward, 1939, p. 41

So great is the power and communion of love that there's an unimaginable level of communion of love that's possible for believers and nonbelievers; it's kinda hard for us to believe. Kinda like what we saw regardin us bein renewed in love by Love that causes Love to sing. JPII talked about a suprisin solidarity that's the result of the communion of love: "In the humiliated and suffering Christ believers and nonbelievers can admire a surprising solidarity, which binds him to our human condition beyond all imaginable measure" (April 22, 2001, Divine Mercy Sunday).

A communion of love and of life.

It is urgent to rediscover and to set forth once more the authentic reality of the Christian faith, which is not simply a set of propositions to be accepted with intellectual assent. Rather, faith is a lived knowledge of Christ, a living remembrance of his commandments, and a truth to be lived out. A word, in any event, is not truly received until it passes into action, until it is put into practice. Faith is a decision involving one's whole

existence. It is an encounter, a dialogue, a communion of love
and of life between the believer and Jesus Christ, the Way, and
the Truth, and the Life (cf. Jn 14:6). It entails an act of trusting
abandonment to Christ, which enables us to live as he lived (cf.
Gal 2:20), in profound love of God and of our brothers and sisters.

— JPII, VS #88

Jesus said, "If a man loves me he will keep my word, and my Father will love him, and we will come to him and make our home with him" (Jn 14:23). As a result of the truth and love in this text, the Great JPII saw and understood the Church as a mystery of communion, a mystery of the communion of love. In fact, for JPII the Church is the home and school of communion which gives birth to a spirituality of communion. In his great Apostolic Letter *Novo Millennio Inuente* (At the Beginning of the New Millennium) #43, the great JPII singled out the makin of the Church the home and school of communion as "the great challenge facing us in the millennium." This challenge must be taken seriously if we want "to be faithful to God's plan and respond to the world's deepest yearnings." The deepest yearnin of the world is to have love be loved — havin Love be loved is the only way for love of justice and the justice of love to restructure the devastatin effects of the impoverished love of injustice.

A spirituality of communion and sharin joy, sufferin, desires, and needs.

Here too our thoughts could run immediately to the action to be
undertaken, but that would not be the right impulse to follow.
Before making practical plans, we need to promote a spirituality
of communion, making it the guiding principle of education
wherever individuals and Christians are formed, wherever
ministers of the altar, consecrated person, and pastoral workers
are trained, wherever families and communities are being built

up. A spirituality of communion indicates above all the heart's
contemplation of the mystery of the Trinity dwelling in us, and
whose light we must also be able to see shining on the face of
the brothers and sisters around us. A spirituality of communion
also means an ability to think of our brothers and sisters in faith
within the profound unity of the mystical body, and therefore as
"those who are part of me." This makes us able to share their
joys and sufferings, to sense their desires and attend to their
needs to offer them deep and genuine friendship.

For JPII, the vitality and youthfulness of the Church depends on each person's link with Christ, each person's communion with Christ. It's through each person's personal communion with Christ that the unity of community is possible with the infinitely broad and expanded Love of the Father. In John 14:2, Jesus says, "In my Father's house are many rooms; if it were not so, would I have told you that I go to prepare a place for you?" The awesomeness of this expanded and ever-expandin reality of the "many rooms" of the Father's house is how the reality of the communion of love breaks out into the world. A true sense of pluralism can also be an expression of this love. However, a false pluralism can threaten and break the unity of communion with the impoverishin factor that's rooted in a lack of fullness of faith and love: "There is no question of breaking or limiting legitimate plurality of expression in spirituality, piety or theological schools. But all this must be an expression of the fullness of faith and not of its poverty" (JPII to German Bishops, November 18, 1980).

The Church is essentially a mystery of communion.

The Church is essentially a mystery of communion: I would
say she is an invitation to communion, to life in communion.
In vertical and horizontal communion; in communion with

God Himself, with Christ and in communion with the other.
Communion explains the full relation of person to person:
a communion intimate and constantly renewed with the
Holy Trinity who is the very source of life, communion of life.
Of imitation of Jesus Christ, Redeemer of man, who unites
us closely with God; from whom pours forth the authentic
and active communion of love among us, by reason of our
ontological resemblance with him.

— JPII, March 31, 1979, to "Communion and Liberation"

As Cardinal George said in his dissertation on culture in the teachings of JPII, "When relationships are extended and when actions unite across cultural boundaries, new ways of understanding develop" (*Inculturation and Ecclesial Communion — Culture and Church in the Teaching of Pope John Paul II*, Urbaniana University Press, Rome, 1990, p. 356). The communion of love gives rise to new ways of understandin which in turn will create new and radical ways of showin, livin, expressin, doin, and bein love in a way that involves everybody excludin no one. JPII, the night before undergoin a major surgery said to a sick person, "I am entrusting the Church to you." JPII was not always comfortable with sick people. He honestly and courageously admits, "When I was young, sick people used to intimidate me." André Frossard, who was a close friend of JPII's and conducted a great interview with him, said, "I think that in his own way of looking at things, the Holy Father considers every sick person to be *ipso facto* a kind of sacrament" [JPII and disabled as icons, etc.] (cf. André Frossard, *A Portrait of John Paul II*, p. 68).

◯ne who does not persevere in charity is not saved.

Even though incorporated into the Church, one who does not however persevere in charity is not saved. He remains indeed in the bosom of the Church, but "in body" not "in heart." All children of the Church should nevertheless remember that their exalted condition results, not from their own merits, but from the grace of Christ. If they fail to respond, in thought word and deed to that grace, not only shall they not be saved, but they shall be the more severely judged.

— JPII, *Lumen Gentium* #14

Another response to the provocation "u got 2 love" is rooted in the teachin of the Church that's very challenging. If a person doesn't persevere in charity, that person will not be saved. That's right! So u really got 2 love. Perseverin in the communion of love is rooted in our destiny to be happy with a happiness that is beyond the reach of earthly trials. This doesn't mean that we won't have issues, it means that the issues will not prevail against us; it doesn't mean that we won't experience darkness, it means that the darkness will not overcome us; it doesn't mean we won't get beat down by others or by the events of life or fall all on our own, it means that when these things happen we'll get back up with the unstoppable bounce-back power of love that is stronger than death.

Destined for happiness beyond the reach of earthly trials.

The church, instructed by divine revelation, affirms that man has been created by God for a destiny of happiness beyond the reach of earthly trials.... God has called man, and still calls him to be united in his whole being in perpetual communion with himself in the immortality of the divine life.... This is true not only of Christians but also of all men of good will in whose heart grace is invisibly at work. Since Christ died for all men, and the ultimate vocation of man is in fact one, that is, a divine vocation, we must hold that the Holy Spirit offers to all the possibility of being united with this Paschal mystery in a way known only to God. Such is the great mystery of man enlightening believers through the Christian revelation.

— GS #18, 22

The communion of love requires cultural development and vigilance, accompanied by constant discernment so that the gift of culture given for the exaltation and development of man won't turn against him. B16 on June 15, 2007, for the 25th anniversary of the Pontifical Council For Culture said, "It is therefore even more urgent for the Church to promote cultural development, targeting the human and spiritual quality of its message and content, since culture today is also inevitably affected by globalization which, unless constantly accompanied by vigilant discernment, can turn against man, ending by impoverishing him instead of enriching him. And what great challenges evangelization has to face in this field!"

Everything is contained in this one act of love which embraces God and humanity.

Everything taught by the Law and the Prophets is summed up — he says — in the command. "You shall love the Lord your God with all your heart, and with all your soul, and with all your mind.... You shall love your neighbor as yourself" (Mt 22:37-40). This is everything — the whole faith is contained in this one act of love which embraces God and humanity. Yet now further questions arise: how are we to love God with all our mind, when our intellect can barely reach him? How are we to love him with all our heart and soul, when our heart can only catch a glimpse of him from afar, when there are so many contradictions in the world that would hide his face from us? This is where the two ways in which God has "abbreviated" his

Word come together. He is no longer distant. He is no longer unknown. He is no longer beyond the reach of our heart. He has become a child for us, and in so doing he has dispelled all doubt. He has become our neighbor, restoring in this way the image of man, whom we often find so hard to love. For us, God has become a gift. He has given himself. He has entered time for us. He who is the Eternal One, above time, he has assumed our time and raised it to himself on high.

— B16, December 24, 2007

---

24. School of Love

May I progress passionately and powerfully in your school of love.

Bless me most loving Jesus, Bless me and have mercy on me in the loving kindness of your most gracious heart. My soul chooses to know nothing apart from you, that disciplined by your grace and instructed by the anointing of your Spirit, I may progress well, passionately and powerfully in the school of your love.

— Gertrude of Helfta, *In the School of Love*, p. 102

The foundation of learnin somethin about love in the all important school of love has less to do with "what to do" than with "who do I belong to." The followin from St. John's first letter makes this point shockingly clear: "By this it may be seen who are the children of God, and who are the children of the devil: whoever does not do right is not of God, nor he who does not love his brother" (1 Jn 3:10). And of course, "his brother" means "everybody." Doin right and lovin everybody is a simple and basic summary of why "u got 2 love." However, this basic summary is more complicated to do durin these postmodern days of the new millennium. This is particularly true in light of the culture of relativism and all the many other impoverishin and confusin cultural energies raging today.

We learn to love through Love awakenin love within us by hearin our voice in the steadfast love of Love. It's here, not the here of a place but of a process, the process of Love awakenin with us a new identity — the gradual comin to know ourselves as definitively and infinitely loved. The first school of love is the family. The interaction between a mother and her child becomes the earliest moments when love is awakened in the child. As a mother awakens her child to love, the child comes to know him- or herself as one who is loved. When we enroll ourselves and engage ourselves more fully in the school of Love, our capacity for the fullness of love becomes more readily accessible.

L ove awakened in through a smile.

After a mother has smiled at her child for many days and weeks, she finally receives her child's smile in response. She has awakened love in the heart of her child, and as the child awakens to love, it also awakens to knowledge.... God interprets himself to man as love in the same way: he radiates love, which kindles the light of love in the heart of man, and it is precisely this light that allows man to perceive this love.

— von B, *Love Alone Is Credible*, Ignatius, 2004, p. 76

One of the big lessons we come to learn is how to recognize and turn away from the illusion of *self-sufficiency*. This lesson goes way back to the beginning with Adam, who while turnin in on himself turned away from Love. Yet, precisely in this impoverishin turnin away from Love, Love reveals the fullness of the redeemin and transformin strength of Love by which we overcome the illusion of self-sufficiency.

L ove rejected in the illusion of self-sufficiency.

From its very origins, mankind, seduced by the lies of the Evil One, rejected God's love in the illusion of a self-sufficiency that is impossible (cf. Gen 3:1-7). Turning in on himself, Adam withdrew from that source of life who is God himself, and became the first of "those who through fear of death were subjected to lifelong bondage" (Heb 2:15). God, however, did not give up. On the contrary, man's "no" was the decisive impulse that moved Him to manifest His love in all of its redeeming strength.

— B16, Lent 2007

JPII in CL #34 refers to the "vital synthesis" between the Gospel and culture that helps us and all humanity to know we are definitively loved. This knowledge creates the realistic possibility for us to engage fully and fruitfully in the lovin pursuit of Christ:

> *This vital synthesis will be achieved when the lay faithful know how to put the Gospel and their daily duties of life into a most shining and convincing testimony, where, not fear but the loving pursuit of Christ and adherence to him will be the factors determining how a person is to live and grow, and these will lead to new ways of living more in conformity with human dignity. Humanity is loved by God! This very simple yet profound proclamation is owed to humanity by the Church. Each Christian's words and life must make this proclamation resound: God loves you, Christ came for you, Christ is for you "the way, the truth and the life"! (Jn 14:6).*

To be enkindled in love requires love to wound.

God's purpose is to so enkindle us in love that we are full of life and full of delight. But first, in order to penetrate into our souls, it is necessary for love to wound.

— St. John of the Cross, *Living Flame of Love*, Stanza 1

One of the most bewilderin lessons of love is to discover the necessity of love to wound. St. John of the Cross teaches us that "the property of love is to make the lover equal to the object loved" ("Collected Works," Kavanaugh, 1979, *Magnificat*, Vol. 8, No. 3, 6th Sunday of Easter, p. 301). As B16 said, our definition of love must begin from the wounded pierced side of Christ Crucified (cf. DCE #12). Thus, the mystery and destiny of the human person is rooted in this wound of love. On a Trinity Sunday B16 said, "Love is always a mystery....God is not solitude but perfect communion. For this reason God is not solitude but perfect communion. For this reason the human person, the image of God, realizes himself or herself in love, which is a sincere gift of self."

All lessons learned in the school of love begin and end with the sincere gift of self. This is the essence of the most essential lesson in this school which aims to instruct us to be equipped for perfect communion. This perfection of communion must be lived every day in the everyday world, otherwise it ain't real; and if love ain't real, we won't be able to persevere in charity; and if we don't persevere in charity, we won't be saved.

If the Church is not livin in the everyday world, she might as well not live at all.

Should I be speaking out on matters in the secular world? Should the Church play that role, or should the Church remain within the Church? Do I feel compelled to thrust myself into the secular world of everyday living in New York?... If the Church is not living in the everyday world, then it might as well not live at all. That's what we're here for.

— Cardinal John O'Connor, from *John Cardinal O'Connor*, by Nat Hentoff, Charles Schribners and Sons, NY, 1987, p. 245, from a WCBS radio speech, New York, December 21, 1987

On Christmas Eve of 2006, B16 painted a wonderfully beautiful picture of how God made himself small for us. Love comes to us as a baby to take away our fear of the greatness of love, the fear of the greatness of the gift as well as the fear of the greatness of the demands of love, to make the greatest and most difficult lessons of love doable. Love asks for our love, and at the end of the day wants nothin other from us than our love. The reason why Love wants nothin other from us than our love is because through Love's wantin our love, we learn the greatest lesson in the school of love — we spontaneously learn how to enter into what he feels, thinks, and wills. We learn to live with love and practice the humility of renunciation which belongs to the very essence of love.

*G*od wants nothin other than our love.

God's sign is the baby. God's sign is that he makes himself small for us. This is how he reigns. He does not come with power and outward splendor. He comes as a baby — defenseless and in need of our help. He does not want to overwhelm us with his strength. He takes away our fear of his greatness. He asks for our love: so he makes himself a child. He wants nothing other from us than our love, through which we spontaneously learn to enter into his feelings, his thoughts and his will — we learn to live with him and to practice with him that humility of renunciation that belongs to the very essence of love. God made himself small so that we could understand him, welcome him, and love him.

— B16, December 24, 2006

25. The Great JPII

He extended the glory of his people.
Like a giant he put on his breastplate;
he girded on his armor of war and waged battles,...
He was like a lion in his deeds,...
and deliverance prospered by his hand....
and his memory is blessed for ever....
He was renowned to the ends of the earth;
he gathered in those who were perishing.

I have to practice restraint here so I don't attempt to write a spiritual biography of my hero — which, by the way, I have in the works! Anyway, I was prayin with the Scriptures this mornin while workin on this section, and I was led to the above Scripture about Judas called Maccabeus taken from 1 Maccabees 3:1-9. As I read them, I saw JPII: extendin the glory of his beloved Poland; like a giant puttin on the breastplate of deep interior prayer and communion with Love; like a lion with his deeds in Poland and Rome and across the globe; his memory will be blessed forever, reachin to the ends of the earth as he still gathers in those who are perishin.

The Karol Wojtyla/JPII Polish factor.

It's important to keep in mind what Peter Hebblethwaite refers to as "the Polish factor." He makes an important point to help us get to know JPII better from the inside: *"Memories of the past are not dead facts in a history text book. They remain very much alive and operative, they provide a permanent frame of reference for interpreting the present.... The polish factor affects his thinking.... His whole treatment of Church-State relations, for example, is colored by the story of the martyrdom of St. Stanislaw, one of his predecessors as Archbishop of Krakow"* (The Pope from

Poland, ed. John Whale, Collins, 1980, p. 30). Listen to JPII on June 15, 1999, in Krakow; he's talkin about the flame that was lit from the heroic death of St. Stanislaus and gives us a great taste of the Wojtyla/JPII Polish factor: *"His concern for the Lord's flock, for the lost sheep in need of help, became a model to which the Church in this city for centuries faithfully turned for inspiration. From generation to generation the tradition of unshakable perseverance in respecting God's law and, at the same time showing great love for man was passed on. This tradition came to birth at the tomb of St. Stanislaus.... We turn to the beginnings and to these figures ... to renew our awareness that the roots of the Church in Krakow are profoundly fixed in the Apostolic tradition, prophetic mission and in the witness of martyrdom. Thanks to this point of reference it stayed in close union with the universal Church."*

Elio Guerriero got JP's death right when he said, "His death was the ultimate act of love offered to God on behalf of Christians, other believers, and all people" (*Let Me Go to the Father's House*, Pauline Books and Media, Boston, 2006, p. vii). Cardinal Dziwisz, the longtime faithful secretary and friend of the great JPII reminds us of the great desire Karol Wojtyla had from the very beginnin of his life as Pope John Paul II. The day after his election, JPII expressed with great determination the desire for his new ministry to be a ministry of love: "...from this very minute, a ministry of love in all its manifestations and expressions." As the Cardinal commented, from first-hand experience, "This desire was continually realized before our eyes" (*Let Me Go*, p. 3).

The Cardinal teaches us about JPII what we have see displayed so clearly and heroically: followin the example of Jesus, JPII was full of love, lovin all people, *"embracing with his greatest love those people who are sad and suffering"* (p. 4). Cardinal Ratzinger/B16 on October 16, 2003, for the twenty-fifth anniversary of JP's election made some key points about JP's life. Cardinal Dziwisz sees these points as describin very well *the attitude of love* that *shaped the pastoral style of John Paul II.* Here's a summary of most of them:

- JPII tirelessly traveled the world to bring the Gospel of the love of God made flesh in Jesus Christ.
- JPII always demonstrated — following the example of Jesus Christ — a special love for the poor and the defenseless, bringin to all a spark of truth and love of God.
- Like St. Paul, JPII was enamored (= inflamed with love) of mankind and desired to make them partake not only of the Gospel, but of his very life (cf. 1 Thess 2:5-8).
- JPII took upon himself criticism and injury, but had roused gratitude and love and brought down the walls of hatred and estrangement.
- JPII placed himself entirely at the service of the Gospel, permittin himself to be consumed (2 Cor. 12:15)
- In the life of JPII the word "cross" was not merely a word. JPII let himself be wounded by the cross in soul and body.
- Like St. Paul, JPII also bore sufferin in order to make up in his earthly life, for the Body of Christ, the Church, what is still lackin in the sufferings of Christ (Col 1:24) (*Let Me Go*, pp. 4-5).

Cardinal Dziwisz quotes from a pastoral letter written to the sick and sufferin by Archbishop Wojtyla/JPII on March 8, 1964. Just a few lines are enough for us to see and feel the depths of great love burnin deep within the great JPII. He firmly believed that sufferin, lived with and for Christ, has a great redemptive value that can enrich the entire community of the Church and the world. Here's an excerpt from the letter:

I make extensive use of this truth in my life…. If someone were to ask me what the foundation is for my pastoral ministry in the Archdiocese of Krakow, I would say that to a great extent it is based upon the truth that suffering, the trials through which many of our brothers and sisters pass … is a good. This is what the Lord Jesus taught us; although suffering is an evil, for Christ and in Christ it is a good…. So, then, remember that you are like him, that we all want to become like him, watching you and drawing from you. (Let Me Go, p. 9)

JP's love continued to overflow to the sick durin one of his many pastoral visits. Archbishop Wojtyla/JPII said, "We look upon you with love … we want to witness this love to you in our Christian community" (*Let Me Go*, p. 10).

On the wall facin JP's bed: the sufferin Christ.

On the wall facing the Holy Father's bed was a painting of the suffering Christ bound with ropes, the Ecce Homo, which John Paul gazed upon intently all through his illness.

— Cardinal Dziwisz, Let Me Go, p. 38

Once again, Cardinal Dziwisz shows us the great love for the sick and sufferin in the great heart of the great JPII: "The sick had a firm place in his interior life and were always present in his thoughts. 'You already know,' he said to the sick in Pompeii on October 21, 1979, 'that the pope, in imitation of Jesus, whose Vicar he is on earth, has a special love for the sick and the suffering; consider this particular attention as one of the highest duties of his pastoral ministry'" (*Let Me Go*, pp. 12-13). Driven by the love of Christ, all of JPII's apostolic voyages were entrusted to the prayers and sacrifices of people who were sufferin. This radical and amazin love in the life of this great man and pope is clearly seen in his magnificent description of the disabled person who has a unique role in helpin us learn somethin about love: *"They can teach everyone about the love that saves us; they can become heralds of a new world, no longer dominated by force, violence and aggression, but by love, solidarity and acceptance, a new world transfigured by the light of Christ, the Son of God who became incarnate, who was crucified and rose for us."*

Disabled persons teach everyone about the love that saves.

The disabled person, with all the limitations and suffering that scar him or her, forces us to question ourselves, with respect and wisdom, on the mystery of man. In fact, the more we move about in the dark and unknown areas of human reality, the better we understand that it is in the more difficult and disturbing situations that the dignity and grandeur of the human being emerges. The wounded humanity of the disabled challenges us to recognize, accept and promote in each one of these brothers and sisters of ours the incomparable value of the human being created by God.... Justice calls for continual and loving attention to the lives of others and a response to the special and different needs of every individual, taking into consideration his or her abilities and limitations.... The mentally handicapped need perhaps more attention, affection, understanding and love than any other sick person: they cannot be left alone, unarmed and defenseless, as it were, in the difficult task of facing life.... In this regard, the care of the emotional and sexual dimensions of disabled persons deserves special attention.... The premise for the emotional-sexual education of disabled persons is inherent in the conviction that their need for love is at least as great as anyone else's. They too need to love and to be loved; they need tenderness, closeness and intimacy.... To show disabled persons that we

*love them means showing them that we value them. Attentive
listening, understanding their needs, sharing their suffering,
patience in guidance, are some of the ways to introduce the
disabled into a human relationship of communion, to enable
them to perceive their own value and make them aware of
their capacity for receiving and giving love.... There is no
doubt that in revealing the fundamental frailty of the human
condition, the disabled person becomes an expression of the
tragedy of pain. In this world of ours that approves hedonism
and is charmed by ephemeral and deceptive beauty, the
difficulties of the disabled are often perceived as a shame or a
provocation and their problems as burdens to be removed or
resolved as quickly as possible. Disabled people are, instead,
living icons of the crucified Son. They reveal the mysterious
beauty of the One who emptied himself for our sake and made
himself obedient unto death. They show us, over and above all
appearances, that the ultimate foundation of human existence
is Jesus Christ. It is said, justifiably so, that disabled people are
humanity's privileged witnesses. They can teach everyone about
the love that saves us; they can become heralds of a new world,
no longer dominated by force, violence and aggression, but by
love, solidarity and acceptance, a new world transfigured by the
light of Christ, the Son of God who became incarnate, who was
crucified and rose for us.... God is always on the side of the
lowly, the poor, the suffering and the marginalized. By making
himself human and being born in the poverty of a stable,
the Son of God proclaimed in himself the blessedness of the
afflicted and shared — in all things save sin — the destiny of
man, created in his image. After Calvary, the Cross, embraced
with love, becomes the way of life. It teaches each one of
us that if we know how to travel with abandoned trust the
exhausting, uphill road of human suffering, the joy of the Living
Christ which surpasses every desire and every expectation will
blossom for us and for our brothers and sisters.*

— JPII, January 5, 2004, to the participants in the
International Symposium on the Dignity and Rights
of the Mentally Disabled Person

In an article, "The Greatest Man of Our Time: John Paul II as a Historical Figure," by Adam Schwartz (*Faith and Reason: The Journal of Christendom College*, Spring 2006, Vol. XXI, No.1, pp. 57-62), we read how on the evening of Pope John Paul's burial, historian Timothy Garton Ash declared "today we have witnessed the funeral of the greatest man of our time." Schwartz concluded, "As Ash is a self-described 'agnostic-liberal,' his assessment was not pious hyperbole but rather a clear-eyed appraisal of the pope's stature." Along these lines, Erasmo described JPII as one of the boldest prophets of authentic divine love in a world filled with forgeries, a world where specialization, pragmatism, and self-promotion have become the normal order of life (*Love's Sacred Orders*, p. 29). B16 reminds us that his great predecessor was animated by a "passion for man." His great passion for man is rooted in and overflows with the torrential and lavishin love that unceasingly flows from the great Passion of the God-Man. This explosion of love was triggered by the tragic assassination attempt on his life on May 13, 1981. JPII said, "God has permitted that I too should feel in my flesh suffering and weakness. I invite you to offer with me your trials to the Lord, who realizes great things through the Cross" (July 19, 1981, Gemelli Hospital — a forty-minute telecast to the Eucharistic Congress in Lourdes).

I would like this message of comfort and hope to reach all.

It is by watching Christ and following him with patient trust that we are able to understand how every form of human pain contains within itself a divine promise of salvation and glory. I would like this message of comfort and hope to reach all, especially those experiencing moments of difficulty, those who suffer in body and spirit.

— JPII, Angelus, February 27, 2005

JPII continues to serve the Church and all humanity from the hospital.

Even here in the hospital, in the midst of other sick people ... I continue to serve the Church and all of humanity.

— JPII, Angelus, February 6, 2005

On July 12, 1992, sufferin wound up takin a prominent place in JP's life with a tumor in his large intestine that would require surgery. Cardinal Dziwisz devotedly reports with great love, "This time it showed its true face and was even more striking. John Paul II, who was for many the symbol of physical vigor and untiring activity, suddenly presented himself to the world as a man tried by illness, as a big brother whose health, in spite of his natural robustness, was now weakened by fatigue and by the trials of the years gone by." Cardinal Dziwisz reveals that when someone from JPII's inner circle talked about the sufferin involved in his surgery, JPII replied, "The Church needs suffering." And again, "What are my sufferings compared with the sufferings of Jesus" (*Let Me Go*, pp. 27-28).

From a prayer written by mother Teresa for JPII and his 1992 surgery.

O Lord, once again you have wanted our Pope John Paul II beside you on the cross, to remind the world that only in the cross is there resurrection and life.... Under the weight of the cross, the pope, following the example of Jesus, teaches us to "love" the cross. The Christian's cross is always a holy cross: teach us, O Lord, to stand beneath the wood of the cross. After the cross, O Lord, comes the radiant dawn of the resurrection. Our Holy Father saw this dawn of the resurrection in May of

1981, after he lived through the dark night of that tragic event. As then, so also today the pope will return to serve the Church, after expressing his love for it once again at the foot of the cross.

— L'Osservatore Romano, August 24, 1992, p. 1

Writin a letter to a friend, the great JPII when still Cardinal Wojtyla revealed the renunciation necessary for love to break out into its torrential fullness: "The more love a person wants to give to others, the more he must renounce the love directed to himself, and the more must he forget about his own personal life" (Cardinal Karol Wojtyla to John Szostak in *The Footsteps of John Paul II*, p. 18). In his last book, JPII shows the livin link with the "new order of love" through the renunciation he spoke about in the letter. The renunciation of the love directed toward oneself is linked with the new order and dimension of love opened up by the sufferin of the Crucified God:

> *The suffering of the Crucified God is not just one form of suffering alongside others.... In sacrificing himself for us all, Christ gave new meaning to suffering, opening up a new dimension, a new order: the order of love.... The passion of Christ on the cross gave a radically new meaning to suffering, transforming it from within.... It is this suffering which burns and consumes evil with the flames of love.... All human suffering, all pain, all infirmity contains within itself a promise of salvation.... Evil is present in the world partly so as to awaken our love, our self-gift in generous and disinterested service to those visited by suffering.... Christ has redeemed the world. "By his wounds we are healed" (Is 53:5). (JPII, Memory and Identity, p. 189ff)*

The last years, months, and weeks of JPII's ministry of love.

The last years, months, and weeks of John Paul II's ministry of love were marked by pain, by the inability to walk, by difficulty in speaking, by the cross that he carried serenely and with extraordinary strength, patience and trust in Christ and his Mother. Through suffering and the cross, the pope participated in the Church's struggle against everything opposed to its mission in the modern world: atheism, religious indifference, secularism, consumerism, the civilization of death. The Holy Father's infirmity revealed more deeply who he was for all people of the world, whom he accompanied with prayer amid his physical weakness, offering expressions of particular closeness and participation.

— Cardinal Stanislaw Diwisz, *Let Me Go to the Father's House*, pp. 31-32

B16 expresses his great love for JPII who is close to him.

The Pope is always close to me through his writings: I hear him and I see him speaking, so I can keep up a continuous dialogue with him. He is always speaking to me through his writings. I even know the origin of some of the texts. I can remember the discussions we had about some of them. So I can continue my conversation with the Holy Father. This nearness to him isn't limited to the words and texts, because behind the texts I hear the pope himself. A man who goes to the Lord doesn't disappear: I believe that someone who goes to the Lord comes even closer to us and I feel he is close to me and I am close to the Lord. **I am near the pope and now he helps me be near the Lord and I try to enter this atmosphere of prayer, of love for our Lord, for our**

Lady, and I entrust myself to his prayers. *So there's a permanent dialogue and we're close to each other in a new way, in a very deep way.*

— B16, October 16, 2005, Interview with Polish Radio

26. Love's Great Lovers

A first step to take in learnin somethin from Love's great lovers requires a step that will be repeated time and time again day by day. The best thing about this step is that it reduces the anxiety and stress of not knowin or carin how long it will take, or how many times might we have to keep takin it. The saints, Love's great lovers, provide us with opportunities to learn somethin about love. St. Francis de Sales (St. Frankie D) identifies and describes this step in light of what he calls a "generous soul." Such a person will hold in high estimation the good gifts that have been provided by Love. Such a soul is "never dismayed" either by "the difficulties of the road" that it has to take or "by the greatness of the work it is called upon to perform." St. Frankie D continues to reveal that this generous soul is neither dismayed "by the length of time that it must give" to the work of Love. Finally, the generous soul is not dismayed "by the delay in the progress of the work undertaken."

That I may feel as far as possible that excessive charity.

Lord Jesus Christ
Two favors I beg of you before I die
The first is that I may, as far as possible,
Feel in my soul and in my body the suffering,
Which you oh gentle Jesus
Sustained in your bitter passion.
The second is this:
That I, as far as possible, may receive in my heart
That excessive charity by which you the Son of God
Was inflamed and which activated you willingly
To suffer so much for us sinners.

— St. Francis of Assisi

All of Love's great lovers, in one way or another, filled space and time with the reality and radical newness of the Gospel. This newness of the Gospel is fully realized in the givin of self which engages love deep in the midst of all the different dimensions of human affairs. Joseph Lortz in an amazing book about St. Francis, *Francis — The Incomparable Saint* (Diseldorf, 1951, p. 44), captures wonderfully the explosive love in the fiery blazin heart of St. Francis, one of Love's great lovers: "The saint's power to attract others — sweeping them up to enthusiastic fervor — has prevailed. This draws attention to the super-human aspect of this incomprehensible explosion of saintly life and to the incomparable power of a heroic love, of the absolute idealism of a heart in which the mystery of the Cross was truly renewed."

The authentic meanin of life is realized in the givin of self.

The Christian can "appreciate and achieve deepest and most authentic meaning of life: namely, that of being a gift which is fully realized in the giving of self" (EV #49) ... the life of Christians, who through faith in the Sacraments are inwardly united with Jesus Christ, is "life in the Spirit." Indeed, the Holy Spirit, poured out in our hearts (cf Gal 4:6), becomes in us and for us "a spring of living water welling up to eternal life" (Jn 4:14).... Christian spirituality does not consist in an effort to protect oneself, as if man could further his overall personal growth and achieve salvation by his own strength. The wounded heart wounded by sin, is healed only by the grace of the Holy Spirit, and only if sustained by this grace can man live as a true son of God. Nor does Christian spirituality consist in becoming "immaterial," disembodied as it were, without responsible involvement in human affairs. Indeed, the Holy Spirit's presence in us far from urging us to seek an alienating "escape" penetrates and moves our entire being: intellect, will, emotions and bodily nature, so that our "new nature" (Eph 4:24) will imbue space and time with the newness of the Gospel.

— JPII, General Audience, October 21, 1998

All of Love's great lovers were swept away by the power of a passionate love that burns with the fire of heroic love and absolute idealism. As EU said, love is a ruthless passion; ruthless in the sense that love never stops cause there's never enough; love is unlimited in self-givin and unlimited in its demand. For Love's great lovers, love was the only attraction that could satisfy their hearts. They burned with great passion which in turn purified the negative effects of the passions. This burnin united the forces and energies of *eros* and *agape* to bring together the many different dimensions of love into the unity of a real and fruitful communion of love.

---

*L*ove — a ruthless passion.

Love is a grave and ruthless passion, unlimited in self-giving and unlimited in demand.

— EU, *Anthology*, p. 35

*P*ure passion purifies the passions for pure love.

The distinction between a great passion and the great troubles caused by "the passions" is a distinction that must be made with the absolute clarity of truth. So to help us learn a very important lesson as we continue to strive to learn something about love, it's absolutely valuable to get the "full scoop" on the distinction between passion and the passions. There's no better help to break it all down for us than the CCC. Here are the major teachins of all the details and distinctions regardin passion and the passions:

1764 The passions are natural components of the human psyche; they form the passageway and ensure the connection between the life of the senses and the life of the mind. Our Lord called man's heart the source from which the passions spring (cf. Mk 7:21).

1772 The principal passions are love and hatred, desire and fear, joy, sadness, and anger.

1773 In the passions, as movements of the sensitive appetite, there is neither moral good nor evil. But insofar as they engage reason and will, there is moral good or evil in them.

1765 There are many passions. The most fundamental passion is love, aroused by the attraction of the good. Love causes a desire for the absent good and the hope of obtaining it; this movement finds completion in the pleasure and joy of the good possessed. The apprehension of evil causes hatred, aversion, and fear of the impending evil; this movement ends in sadness at some present evil, or in the anger that resists it.

2555 Christ's faithful "have crucified the flesh with its passions and desires" (Gal 5:24); they are led by the Spirit and follow his desires.

2339 Chastity includes an *apprenticeship in self-mastery* which is a training in human freedom. The alternative is clear: either man governs his passions and finds peace, or he lets himself be dominated by them and becomes unhappy (cf. Sir 1:22). "Man's dignity therefore requires him to act out of conscious and free choice, as moved and drawn in a personal way from within, and not by blind impulses in himself or by mere external constraint. Man gains such dignity when, ridding himself of all slavery to the passions, he presses forward to his goal by freely choosing what is good and, by his diligence and skill, effectively secures for himself the means suited to this end" (GS 17).

1762 The human person is ordered to beatitude by his deliberate acts: the passions or feelings he experiences can dispose him to it and contribute to it.

1768 Strong feelings are not decisive for the morality or the holiness of persons; they are simply the inexhaustible reservoir of images and affections in which the moral life is expressed. Passions are morally good when they contribute to a good action, evil in the opposite case. The upright will orders the movements of the senses it appropriates to the good and to beatitude; an evil will succumbs to disordered passions and exacerbates them. Emotions and feelings can be taken up into the *virtues* or perverted by the vices.

1766 "To love is to will the good of another" (St. Thomas Aquinas, *STh* I-II, 26, 4, *corp. art.*). All other affections have their source in this first movement of the human heart toward the good. Only the good can be loved (cf. St. Augustine, *De Trin.*, 8, 3, 4: PL 42, 949-950). Passions "are evil if love is evil and good if it is good" (St. Augustine, *De civ. Dei* 14, 7, 2: PL 41, 410).

908 By his obedience unto death (cf. *Phil* 2:8-9), Christ communicated to his disciples the gift of royal freedom, so that they might "by the self-abnegation of a holy life, overcome the reign of sin in themselves" (LG 36):

That man is rightly called a king who makes his own body an obedient subject and, by governing himself with suitable rigor, refuses to let his passions breed rebellion in his soul, for he exercises a kind of royal power over himself. And because he knows how to rule his own person as king, so too does he sit as its judge. He will not let himself be imprisoned by sin, or thrown headlong into wickedness. (St. Ambrose, *Psal. 118*:14:30: PL 15:1476.)

JPII said durin a beatification ceremony on March 7, 1999, that "the saints … drank from the fountain of Christ's love to the point that they were transformed and in turn became overflowing springs to quench the thirst of the many brothers and sisters they met on life's path." The love of Love's great lovers overflowed with the lavish, excessive, and torrential passion of Love that gave expression to a passionate pursuit of quenchin the thirst of others. One of the greatest examples of this love in the postmodern era is Blessed Mother Teresa. She burned with a passionate love that shined in the darkness of the most intense impoverishment of love, the poverty of not bein wanted. She was on fire with love for Jesus and burned with a passionate desire to quench his thirst for love of souls. On every wall in every chapel in every one of her convents around the world was written what was engraved on her heart: *"I thirst"* (Jn 19:28).

The thirst of Christ Crucified became the drivin force of her life. She became a heroic witness to the thirstin love of God. Durin her beatification ceremony on October 19, 2003, JPII acknowledged this passionate thirst in the life and heart of his good friend, as "the inner force that drew her out of herself and made her 'run in haste' across the globe to labor for the sanctification and salvation of the poorest of the poor." B16 basically said the same thing in his April 1, 2007, Palm Sunday/World Youth Day address: "In order to respond instantly to the cry of Jesus, 'I thirst,' a cry that touched her deeply, she began to take in the people who were dying of the streets of Calcutta in India. From that time onward, the only desire of her life was to quench the thirst of love felt by Jesus, not with words, but with concrete action by recognizing his disfigured countenance thirsting for love in the faces of the poorest of the poor.… The message of this humble witness of divine love has spread around the world.

Each one of us, my friends, has been given the possibility of reaching this same level of love, but only by having recourse to the indispensable support of divine Grace."

The great acts and heroisms of God's great lovers.

Let us rejoice in the great adoring acts and splendid heroisms of God's great lovers and humbly do the little we can. We too have our place.

— EU, *Anthology*, p. 123

This awesome heroism of Love's great lovers can be a source of great inspiration for us to learn somethin about love, to learn somethin that will renew and enflame the desire of our hearts to do what we can, so we can have our place and do our part in the great and mysterious designs of Love. Again, we look to Mary the Mother of Love at the foot of the Cross. Monsignor Romero Guardini recalls how Mary experienced Jesus growin further away from her as Jesus moved forward to be lifted high on the Cross. Feelin the pain of this movement of Love, Guardini amazingly points out that "she increased her faith to match his new stature and encompassed him anew…. She received this separation in a final act of sharing his suffering, and once again, in this very act, she stood by him in faith" (Guardini, *The Inner Life of Jesus*).

St. Faustina in her diary, *Divine Mercy in My Soul,* explodes with the boldness of love in a way that is similar to St. Francis. In spite of feelings of her smallness and great misery, she wants to love Jesus as no other human soul has loved him. She helps us big-time to learn somethin about love — to learn not to be afraid, and that with love we can conquer ourselves and our fear.

Even the most miserable soul can become a great saint.

I want to love you as no human soul has ever loved you before; and although I am utterly miserable and small, I have nevertheless cast the anchor of my trust deep down in the abyss of your mercy, O my God and Creator! In spite of my great misery I fear nothing, but hope to sing you a hymn of glory forever. Let no soul, even the most miserable, fall prey to doubt; for as long as one is alive, each one can become a great saint, so great is the power of God's grace. It remains only for us not to oppose God's action.

— St. Faustina, Diary #283

This generosity and boldness of Love's great lovers are also seen in St. Thérèse of Lisieux. For Thérèse, Love was the vocation that included every vocation. She became a great lover of Love as she discovered her mission to be love in the heart of the Church. In her autobiography, *Story of a Soul*, Thérèse said, *"I feel in me the vocation of the Priest. I have the vocation of the Apostle. Martyrdom was the dream of my youth and this dream has grown with me. Considering the mystical body of the Church, I desired to see myself in them all. Charity gave me the key to my vocation. I understood that the Church had a Heart and that this Heart was burning with love. I understood that Love comprised all vocations, that Love was everything, that it embraced all times and places ... in a word, that it was eternal! Then in the excess of my delirious joy, I cried out: O Jesus, my Love ... my vocation, at last I have found it.... My vocation is Love!"*

Thérèse and Love as the vocation which includes every vocation.

The CCC links the burnin heart of Thérèse with the vocation of Love, which includes all and every other vocation. This is how Thérèse discovered her own vocation as bein love in the heart of the Church.

CCC 826: Charity is the soul of the holiness to which all are called: it "governs, shapes, and perfects all the means of sanctification" (LG 42).

If the Church was a body composed of different members, it couldn't lack the noblest of all; *it must have a Heart, and a Heart BURNING WITH LOVE.* And I realized that this love alone was the true motive force which enabled the other members of the Church to act; if it ceased to function, the Apostles would forget to preach the gospel, the Martyrs would refuse to shed their blood. LOVE, IN FACT, IS THE VOCATION WHICH INCLUDES ALL OTHERS; IT'S A UNIVERSE OF ITS OWN, COMPRISING ALL TIME AND SPACE — IT'S ETERNAL! (St. Thérèse of Lisieux, *Autobiography of a Saint*, tr. Ronald Knox [London: Harvill, 1958] 235)

St. Ambrose, like all of Love's great lovers, was aware that "there is ... a stream which flows down on God's saints like a torrent." This stream is the torrent of the love that is lavished upon us all. In John 15:9 Jesus said, "As the Father has loved me, so I have loved you; abide in my love." The insight into these words of Jesus by Adrienne von Speyr helps us penetrate the great mystery of the love that so amazingly swept away the lives of Love's great lovers: "Anyone who is loved only has to let himself be covered by love.... The Apostles, the saints, experienced proofs of his love *continually raining down on them ... and all the Lord requires of them is that they do not draw back from this torrent*" (Adrienne von Speyr, *John*, Vol. 3, Ignatius Press, p. 171).

The somethin we learn here about love is the simple yet difficult task of trustin Love more and more each day so as to let Love purify us, transform us, and enflame us with the fire and energy of the love that goes to the end; to sweep us up and away in a torrent of love so lavishly and incessantly poured out upon us. This will experience us with proofs of love that will in turn make us become proofs of the love we experienced, spurred on by the self-givin love of Love. It's like what B16 said in #8 of SS: "For us who contemplate these figures, their way of acting and living is de facto a 'proof' that the things to come, the promise of Christ, are not only a reality that we await, but a real presence." We can be and are called to become set ablaze as witnesses of the real presence of real love that flows from the very heart of Love.

The saints: wholly aflame realists — selfless and yet wholly a self.

The saints ... are spurred on by God's self-giving to attempt and realize things which those who remain tied to their own resources could never have dreamed of.... The saint ... is wholly aflame.... He burns with an absolute fire; he is selfless and yet wholly a self, a man; he does what others plan to do or deliberately forget.... The saints are true realists; they take seriously the hopelessness of man as it is and do not seek a refuge from the present in the future. They get on with the job in spite of everything and hope against hope. They are clever but not calculating; they live out a desire to squander themselves which stems from God's Eucharistic Love ... and if they are genuine they never point to themselves; they themselves are only a reflection; it is the master of the flame who is all important.

— von B, *Elucidations*

---

27. Love Your Enemies

In Luke 6:27, Jesus unleashes what is more than likely the greatest challenge of all His teachins on love; and at the same time He unleashes the greatest power of Love for us to actually make forward strides in doin it: "Love your enemies." This teachin champions the true revolution of love. On February 18, 2007, in remarks at St. Peter's Square, B16 asked an awesome question about this teachin, which is loaded with both the intensity of the impossibility of this command as well as the intensity of power which makes this command possible. Are you feelin me here?

The question raised by B16 is a testimony to the greatness of the clarity and precision of his great intellect combined with the profundity and depth of his heart and soul. He has one of the most awesome brain/heart combinations in modern times. Here goes his question — check it out: *"Why does Jesus ask us to love precisely our enemies, that is, a love which exceeds human capacities?"* The basic foundation of his answer is seen in what he refers to as *"the nucleus of the Christian revolution."* It's a revolution *"not based on strategies of economic, political, or media power."* Accordin to B16, it's a revolution of love that is founded on a *"love that does not ultimately rely on human resources but is a gift of God which is obtained by trusting solely and unreservedly in his merciful goodness."* It's the new revolutionary "tippin point" for the rebalancin of the heart of the world startin with our own heart.

A love that exceeds our human capacities.

"Love your enemies" (Lk 6:27). Why does Jesus ask us to precisely love our enemies, that is, a love which exceeds human capacities?... Christ's proposal is realistic because it takes into account too much violence, too much injustice,

*and therefore that this situation cannot be overcome except by countering it with more goodness. This "more" comes from God: it is his mercy which was made flesh in Jesus, and which alone can "tip the balance" of the world from evil to good, starting with that small and decisive "world" which is the human heart.... **The attitude of one who is so convinced of God's love and power that he is not afraid to tackle evil with the weapons of love and truth alone** ... the nucleus of the Christian revolution, a revolution not based on strategies of economic, political or media power: the revolution of love, a love that does not ultimately rely on human resources but is a gift of God which is obtained by trusting solely and unreservedly in his merciful goodness. Here is the newness of the Gospel which silently changes the world! Here is the heroism of the lowly who believe in God's love and spread it even at the cost of their lives.*

— B16, February 18, 2007

To look at the world with the eyes of Christ, to love with his heart, think with his mind and serve with his Church will require us to expect "nothing in return" (Lk 6:35). Lovin our enemies depends upon the release and development of our capacity to love beyond our natural capacity; to be engaged in the perfection of the Father, even "as your heavenly Father is perfect" (Mt 5:48); and "merciful, even as your Father is merciful" (Lk 6:35). The panorama of this perfection involves bein generous and good to the ungrateful and the selfish. Not an easy thing; it will require learnin and re-learnin the obedience of Jesus, learnin obedience from what we suffer in faith workin through love.

This lovin our enemies requires us to become a new creation, to be made new again and again by Love. Our task in this renewin process is makin sure self-interest is not left unchallenged. Leavin our self-interest unchallenged is really very easy to do. When self-interest remains unchallenged, it feeds the impoverishin energies of impoverished love that would have us settle for love and life that is less than what it could be. That's because acknowledgin and overcomin our self-interest is really difficult, and yet this self-interest stuff is precisely the stuff that gets transformed by Grace into generous and even heroic levels of self-gift. This is the work of Love, makin love of enemies possible as a result of God, Who is Love, and who continually expands our hearts for the possibilities of more love.

---

*L*ove your enemies.

Love your enemies, and do good, and lend, expecting nothing in return, and your reward will be great, and you will be sons of the Most High; for he is kind to the ungrateful and the selfish. Be merciful as your Father is merciful.

— Luke 6:35

---

28. Social Doctrine of Love

The judgment of God will be based precisely on love.

At the end of the life of every person and at the close of the history of humanity, the judgment of God will be based precisely on love, the practice of justice, and assistance to the poor (cf. Mt 25:31-46).

— JPII, January 10, 2001

The connection of the great tradition of the social doctrine of the Church with culture is crucial. The reality of the demands of love are not just spiritual, emotional, and ecclesial, they are also cultural and social. The love revealed in the Gospel of Jesus makes its lastin effect by impactin our ways of thinkin. Accordin to JPII, the Gospel unleashes the creative power of love that "penetrates profoundly in the culture" (April 27, 2004). This assures our rediscoverin the new and savin order of love — the energy that drives the world. It involves our cooperation with the divine plan of love energizing us to assist and impact the needs and circumstances of real people who have real problems.

Love — the energy that drives the world.

Suzan Rakoczy rightly declares "It is the energy of love that drives the world" (Great Mystics and Social Justice — Walking on the Two Feet of Love, Paulist Press, 2006, p. 206). This drivin energy of love must, accordin to the very nature of love, penetrate the cultural, social, and political

> order. *Rakoczy refers to a "political love." It seems to me what she's sayin goes hand in hand with what Albacete refers to as "the unavoidable political consequences" as the result of experiencin the sacred which unleashes the energy of love that builds a culture of life and love: The experience of the sacred points to a way of life, a culture, that defines a form of relating to and dealing with "others," and as such has unavoidable political consequences (Albacete,* God at the Ritz, *p. 36).*

One of the great and many treasures left to us by the great patrimony of the great JPII is the *Compendium of the Social Doctrine of the Church.* In order for this social doctrine of love to be lived more fully, and rescue the many tragic social circumstances of impoverished love in the cities, towns, and villages across the globe, it's absolutely essential for the transcendent dignity of every human person to be acknowledged and protected. "The new law of love embraces the entire human family and knows no limits since the proclamation of the salvation wrought by Christ extends 'to the ends of the earth' (Acts 1:8)" (*Compendium* #3). As we read in #4 of the *Compendium,* "Discovering that they are loved by God people come to understand their own transcendent dignity." This discovery of bein loved by God is crucial for us to learn somethin about love, to learn not only to be satisfied with ourselves; rather than bein satisfied only with our selves, discoverin ourselves as loved by God frees us to encounter our neighbor in what the *Compendium* calls "a network of relationships that are ever more authentically human." The fruit of this awareness of bein loved, as the *Compendium* puts it, raises up "men and women who are 'made new' by the love of God, and are able to change the roles and the quality of relationships transforming even social structures."

Love faces a vast field of work.

Love faces a vast field of work and the Church is eager to make her contribution with her social doctrine, which concerns the whole person and is addressed to all people.

— *Compendium* #5

The social doctrine of Love has been given to raise up saints who are committed to makin a social and cultural impact. On October 29, 2004, in an address to the Pontifical Council for Justice and Peace, JPII expressed his conviction that the time has come for a "new season of social holiness." It's the time for saints who are committed to makin a difference in social and cultural life: "It is the hour of a new season of social holiness, of saints who manifest to the world and in the world the perennial and inexhaustible fecundity (= fruitfulness or productiveness) of the Gospel." JPII referred to the Compendium as "an instrument capable of helping Christians in their daily commitment to make the world more just, in the evangelical perspective of an authentic, solidaristic humanism."

The social doctrine of the Church opens the horizons of charity.

At a time like ours, marked by the globalization of the social question, the Church invites all to recognize and affirm the centrality of the human being in all realms and in all manifestations of a social character.... The social doctrine of the Church implores you especially, lay Christians, to live in society as a witness of Christ Savior that opens horizons of charity. This is the hour of charity, including social and political charity, able to illuminate with the grace of the Gospel human realities of work, economy, politics, building paths of peace, justice and friendship among peoples.

— JPII, October 29, 2004

The world is bathed in the light of absolute love.

However profane the world may be in its actions and attitudes, it is bathed in the sacral light of absolute love, which not only illuminated it externally but penetrates its innermost resources.... The Christian lives in the sphere of an event that signifies absolute love — that is, in a boundless realm beyond which nothing greater can be imagined. If one tries to, he falls into a void that eventually destroys the man who was created for something greater than the world we know.

— von B, *The Moment of Christian Witness*, Communio Books, Ignatius Press, 1994, pp. 54-55

The world is bathed in the light of absolute love. The event of this love places demands on us that require our response. The social doctrine of Love has been given to ensure that we live the justice dimension of love. As JPII said, "At the end of the life of every person and at the close of the history of humanity, the judgment of God will be based precisely on love, the practice of justice, and assistance to the poor" (cf. Mt 25:31-46). This doctrine is a rather weak and unknown and not-too-much-talked-about part of the fullness of the Catholic faith. Why? Cause it will most certainly ignite a fire and awaken slumberin consciences. If our conscience is alive and correctly formed, it will leave us restless until we do somethin with love to make a difference in the life of somebody. Then we will become more of who we were created to be, so we can do what we were created to do — namely love. It's so much easier to stay in our comfort zone — it's easy to love the ease of not bein challenged.

We cannot pass over in silence the presence in our midst.

How many single mothers are struggling to take care of their children! How many old people there are who are abandoned and without means to live! In institutions for orphans and abandoned children there is no lack of those without enough food and clothing. How can we fail to mention the sick, who cannot be given proper care because of a lack of resources? On the streets and in the squares the number of homeless people is increasing. We cannot pass over in silence the presence in our midst of all these brothers and sisters, who are also members of the mystical body of Christ.

— JP, Poland, June 2, 1997

In #14 of DCE, B16 said, "A Eucharist which does not pass over into the concrete practice of love is intrinsically fragmented." A fragmented Eucharist is the result of an impoverished love that does not feel and act in a responsible way. In the same way that love is fractured when *eros* and *agape* is not united, so too suffers the social doctrine of love when love is separated from justice. The fundamental vocation for every person to love must be expressed through our takin care of one another. Archbishop Romero put it well — he put it along the same lines as B16 — when he said that a love that did not demand justice would be a caricature of love.

Christian love leads to commitment to cultural and social projects.

Christian love leads to denunciation, proposals and a commitment to cultural and social projects. Humanity is coming to understand ever more clearly that it is linked by one sole destiny that requires joint acceptance of responsibility, a responsibility shared by an integral and shared humanism.

— *Compendium #6*

A civilization of love that did not demand justice would not be a true civilization.

A civilization of love that did not demand justice of people would not be a true civilization: it would not delineate genuine human relations. It is a caricature of love to try to cover over with alms what is lacking in justice, to patch over with an appearance of benevolence when social justice is missing. True love begins by demanding what is just in the relations of those who love.

— Archbishop Oscar Romero, April 12, 1979

29. Civilization of Love

The civilization of love is not based on some kind of pathetic revision of "utopia." The civilization of love is somethin given from beyond that requires generosity and courage, here and now, with regard to our accomplishin the designs of Love that flow from Love's fullness. It's based upon the human capacity for "transcendence," our ability to go beyond ourselves, to make a gift of ourselves. The civilization of love originates in the revelation of God who is love and is inseparably linked to the family.

The civilization of love/the culture of love.

Etymologically the word "civilization" is derived from "civis" — "citizen," and it emphasizes the civic or political dimension of the life of every individual. But the most profound meaning of the term "civilization" is not merely political, but rather pertains to human culture. Civilization belongs to human history because it answers man's spiritual and moral needs. Created in the image and likeness of God, man has received the world from the hands of the Creator, together with the task of shaping it in his own image and likeness. The fulfillment of this task gives rise to civilization, which in the final analysis is nothing else than the "humanization of the world." In a certain sense civilization means the same thing as "culture." And so one could also speak of the "culture of love," even though it is preferable to keep to the now familiar expression. The civilization of love, in its current meaning, is inspired by the words of the conciliar Constitution Gaudium et Spes: "Christ ... fully discloses man to himself and unfolds his noble calling." And so we can say that the civilization of love originates in the revelation of the God who "is love," as John writes (1 Jn 4:8, 16); it is effectively described by Paul in the hymn of charity found in his First Letter to the Corinthians (13:1-13). This civilization is intimately linked to the love "poured into our hearts through the Holy Spirit which has been given to us" (Rom 5:5), and it grows as a result of the constant cultivation which the Gospel allegory of the vine and the branches describes in such a direct way: "I am the true vine, and my Father is the vinedresser. Every branch of mine that bears no fruit, he takes away, and every branch that does bear fruit he prunes, that it may bear more fruit" (Jn 15:1-2). In the light of these and other texts of the New Testament it is possible to understand what is meant by the "civilization of love," and why the family is organically linked to this civilization.

— JPII, *Letter to Families* #13

In EV #6, JPII makes an urgent appeal for an authentic civilization of truth and life. His appeal is rooted in the work of love that brings together justice and solidarity as well as an increase of the energies and fruits of this indispensable union: "To all the members of the Church, the people of life and for life, I make this most urgent appeal, that together we may offer this world of ours new signs of hope, and work to ensure that justice and solidarity will increase and that a new culture of human life will be affirmed, for the building of an authentic civilization of truth and love."

Through the free gift of self man finds himself.

The concept of alienation needs to be led back to the Christian vision of reality, by recognizing in alienation a reversal of means and ends. When man does not recognize in himself and in others the value and grandeur of the human person, he effectively deprives himself of the possibility of benefiting from his humanity and of entering into that relationship of solidarity and communion with others for which God created him. Indeed, it is through the free gift of self that man truly finds

*himself (Gaudium et Spes #24). This gift is made possible
by the human person's essential "capacity for transcendence."
Man cannot give himself to a purely human plan for reality, to
an abstract ideal or to a false utopia. As a person, he can give
himself to another person or to other persons, and ultimately
to God, who is the author of his being and who alone can fully
accept his gift. A man is alienated if he refuses to transcend
himself and to live the experience of self-giving and of the
formation of an authentic human community oriented towards
his final destiny, which is God. A society is alienated if its forms
of social organization, production and consumption make
it more difficult to offer this gift of self and to establish this
solidarity between people.*

— JPII, CA #41

Again we come to the all-important necessity for self-transcendence. There is no workin towards buildin the civilization of love without it. Without self-transcendence we deprive our humanity of the possibility of bein enriched with the fullness of love. Lack of self-transcendence makes strong the strongholds of impoverished love, keepin people and cultures alienated and runnin away from each other in fear, rather than workin together to build up love. As EU points out, this transcendence penetrates the natural order with the supernatural power of love. And even if and when we achieve justice in the social order, if we have not love, it's nothin! Well, let me take that back and qualify it in light of C.S. Lewis, who says in *The Problem of Pain*, "What is outside the system of self-giving is not earth, nor nature, nor 'ordinary life' but simple and solely hell ... that fierce imprisonment in the self." It's not about bein politically correct, it's not some type of moralism, nor is it about maintainin some lukewarm, status quo, business-as-usual kind of affair. EU puts it like this: "Though we achieve social justice, liberty, peace itself; though we give our bodies to be burned for these admirable causes, if we lack charity we are nothing. For the Kingdom is the Holy, not the moral; the Beautiful not the correct; the Perfect not the adequate; charity not law" (EU, *Anthology*, p. 58).

The civilization of love brings together all the different forms of love which are brought into existence and sustained by the Love present in the Eucharist. The strength to work tirelessly in buildin this civilization is contained in the food of truth: "The food of truth — the Eucharist — demands that we denounce inhumane situations in which people starve to death because of injustice and exploitation, and it gives us renewed strength and courage to work tirelessly in the service of the civilization of love" (B16, *Sacramentum Caritatis* #90). This renewed strength and courage to work tirelessly in denouncin inhumane situations and buildin up the new civilization of love will also prepare us for makin radical renouncements by embracin the logic of sharin and solidarity.

ℬe prepared to make radical renouncements.

When the logic of sharing and solidarity prevails, it is possible to correct the course and direct it to a fair development for the common good of all. Basically, it is a matter of choosing between selfishness and love, between justice and dishonesty and ultimately, between God and Satan. If loving Christ and one's brethren is not to be considered as something incidental and superficial but, rather, the true and ultimate purpose of our whole existence, it will be necessary to know how to make basic choices, to be prepared to make radical renouncements, if necessary even to the point of martyrdom. Today, as yesterday, Christian life demands the courage to go against the tide, to love like Jesus, who even went so far as to sacrifice himself on the Cross.

— B16, October 3, 2007

Every little sacrifice counts in givin meanin to the civilization of love and makin it real. As the great JPII said, "The sacrifices which you make, however small, will save bodies and bring fresh life to souls, and the expression 'civilization of love' will no longer be devoid of meaning" (JPII, Lent 1986). These sacrifices and radical renouncements will contribute to the buildin of a new culture by helpin people feel included, and bein healed from the wounds of bein excluded. This is very basic and very important for makin love happen in a way that makes a difference. JPII in EV #98 talks about this kink of mobilization for a new culture:

> In this mobilization for a new culture of life no one must feel excluded: everyone has an important role to play. Together with the family, teachers and educators have a particularly valuable contribution to make. Much will depend on them if young people, trained in true freedom, are to be able to preserve for themselves and make known to others new, authentic ideals of life, and if they are to grow in respect for and service to every other person, in the family and in society.

ﬔeeds that strengthen the bases of the civilization of love and life.

Furthermore, how can we fail to mention all those daily gestures of openness, sacrifice and unselfish care which countless people lovingly make in families, hospitals, orphanages, homes for the elderly and other centers or communities which defend life? Allowing herself to be guided by the example of Jesus the "Good Samaritan" (cf. Lk 10:29-37) and upheld by his strength, the Church has always been in the front line in providing charitable help: so many of her sons and daughters, especially men and women Religious, in traditional and ever new forms, have consecrated and continue to consecrate their lives to God, freely giving of themselves out *of love for their neighbor, especially for the weak and needy. These deeds strengthen the bases of the "civilization of love and life," without which the life of individuals and of society itself loses its most genuinely human quality. Even if they go unnoticed and remain hidden to most people, faith assures us that the Father "who sees in secret" (Mt 6:6) not only will reward these actions but already here and now makes them produce lasting fruit for the good of all.*

— JPII, EV #27

Arnold Toynbee came up with a very creative insight into what he calls creative minorities. This is the new cultural creature that can bring together both the many different dimensions of love as well as the many different dimensions of culture. Toynbee describes these creative minorities as follows: "These creative minorities are not fortuitous assemblages of dissident groups, cults, and naysayers, but on the contrary a self-conscious movement of individuals and groups toward a new and purified cultural ideal.... It is they who provide both the prophetic critique of the present and a vision of a new and ideal culture" (Arnold Toynbee, "A Study of History," pp. 91-92, Steven J. Tonsor "What to Do While Awaiting the Apocalypse?: The Role of Creative Minorities in a Time of Cultural Crisis" in *Toward the Renewal of Civilization: Political Order and Culture*, ed. T. William Boxx and Gary M. Quinlivan, Willam B. Eerdmans Pub. Co., Grand Rapids, Michigan, 1998).

Tradition and meetin the ongoin cultural crisis.

Successful creative minorities in the past have always taken from tradition that which is noblest, that which is best, and conformed it to an overriding vision of a better future. It is this prophetic vision of the world made new drawing its substance from the orthodoxy of tradition that will meet the challenge of perennial cultural crisis (Tonsor, p. 100). An example of the exact opposite of what is best from the best of tradition is the arrival of the professional baby-namin business. Yes, sad but true. Friday, June 22, 2007, in the Wall Street Journal, p. 1, an article by Alexandra Alter called "The Baby-Name Business": *As family names and old religious standbys continue to lose favor, parents are spending more time and money on the issue and are increasingly turning to strangers to help.*

In light of the historical and cultural events that have brought down walls and opened up borders, there are still huge gaps between the dream for and reality of justice and love. Yet, there is also an increasin hunger and thirst for a new more human civilization of love. The demands of love are waitin to be embraced by all. In other words, "we got 2 love." These demands will be fulfilled only by, and to the degree that, we come to know ourselves as definitively loved, and express that love with the logic of solidarity and service in makin a sincere gift of ourselves more and more every day.

We all have to respond to the expectations of a new human culture.

Walls have crumbled. Borders have opened. However, enormous barriers still stand between the hopes of justice and their realization, between wealth and wretched poverty, while rivalries are reborn as long as the struggle to possess overrides the respect for the person. An earthly messianism has crumbled and the thirst for a new justice is springing up in the world. A great hope has been born of freedom, responsibility, solidarity, spirituality. Everyone is calling for a new fully human civilization in this privileged hour in which we are living. This immense hope of humanity must not be disappointed: we all have to respond to the expectations of a new human culture.

— JPII, January12, 1990

No communion of persons, no civilization of love.

Yet there is no true love without an awareness that God "is Love" — and that man is the only creature on earth which God has called into existence "for its own sake." Created in the image and likeness of God, man cannot fully "find himself" except through the sincere gift of self. Without such a concept of man, of the person and the "communion of persons" in the family, there can be no civilization of love; similarly, without the civilization of love it is impossible to have such a concept of person and of the communion of persons. The family constitutes the fundamental "cell" of society. But Christ — the "vine" from which the "branches" draw nourishment — is needed so that this cell will not be exposed to the threat of a kind of cultural uprooting which can come both from within and from without. Indeed, although there is on the one hand the "civilization of love," there continues to exist on the other hand the possibility of a destructive "anti-civilization," as so many present trends and situations confirm.

— JPII, *Letter to Families* #13

30. Till the End of Time

I am with you always.

Go therefore and make disciples of all nations, baptizing them in the name of the Father and of the Son and of the Holy Spirit, teaching them to observe all that I have commanded you; and lo, I am with you always, to the close of the age.

— Matthew 28:19-20

Love is a presence, and love stays with us until the end of time. As Jesus is leavin his disciples revealin the mystery of his ascension into Heaven, he promises to be present until the end (Jesus is God — God is Love). Imagine, somebody promisin to be with you till the end as they're leavin you to go to heaven? Strange? On one hand, yes. On the other hand, when that person is God, it's mysterious and marvelous at the same time. Love can be in more than one place at the same time. In fact, love is everywhere all the time, and it's precisely the point Jesus is makin: he will be with us till the end of time, and in the meantime we got 2 love in the sense of goin forth makin disciples. The fundamental dimension of bein a disciple of Jesus is love, it's the essence of the new commandment and of discipleship. Jesus said, "A new commandment I give to you, that you love one another; even as I have loved you, that you also love one another. By this all men will know that you are my disciples, if you have love for one another" (Jn 13:34-35).

Christian culture and the ceaseless effort to widen the frontiers of the Kingdom.

To live for eternal truths, to possess the first fruits of eternal life, while facing every practical responsibility and meeting

the demands of the present moment, and place on their
own ground — that is the spirit by which a Christian culture
lives and is known. For Christian culture involves a ceaseless
effort to widen the frontier of the Kingdom of God — not
only horizontally by increasing the number of Christians, but
vertically by penetrating deeper into human life and bringing
every human activity into closer relations with its spiritual
center.

— Christopher Dawson, *The Historic Reality*
of Christian Culture, p. 20

With Jesus promisin to stay with us till the end of time while he's gettin ready to ascend into heaven creates a vital tension between two worlds. This vital tension is a major contribution of Christian culture to the world. To live for eternal truths while strivin to love here and now, takin care of all the practical details of the complicated reality of a broken world cryin out for love is the key. As Dawson says, this will involve a ceaseless 24/7 nonstop effort to "widen the frontier of the Kingdom of God" — *the Kingdom of Love*. This will be done by the showin of love to one another, as Jesus has commanded.

The very sound of the words "till the end of time" kicks up all kinds of feelings and images. The same is true with the words "eternal life." I really love how B16 in #12 of his encyclical *Spe Salvi* expresses what he feels and thinks about eternal life. He uses his brilliant mind and depth of heart to set us straight. At the end of the day, he thinks it's an inadequate term because it creates confusion. He's very sensitive to how this word sometimes makes people feel afraid, makin them think *"of the life that we know and love and do not want to lose."* He reminds us that eternal life is *"not an unending succession of days in the calendar."* He awesomely tells us it is somethin more like *"a supreme moment of satisfaction.... plunging into the ocean of infinite love, a moment in which time — the before and the after — no longer exists. It's somethin like a plunging ever anew into the vastness of being, in which we are simply overwhelmed with joy."*

Eternal life — plungin into the infinite ocean of love.

Inevitably it is an inadequate term that creates confusion. "Eternal," in fact, suggests to us the idea of something interminable, and this frightens us; "life" makes us think of the life that we know and love and do not want to lose, even though very often it brings more toil than satisfaction, so that while on the one hand we desire it, on the other hand we do not want it. To imagine ourselves outside the temporality that imprisons us and in some way to sense that eternity is not an unending succession of days in the calendar, but something more like the supreme moment of satisfaction, in which totality embraces us and we embrace totality — this we can only attempt. It would be like plunging into the ocean of infinite love, a moment in which time — the before and after — no longer exists. We can only attempt to grasp the idea that such a moment is life in the full sense, a plunging ever anew into the vastness of being, in which we are simply overwhelmed with joy.

— B16, *Spe Salvi* #12

Rather than understandin "end of time" meanin "no more time," I understand it as makin the most of our time. We never know how much time we have left. Even when we don't think of that, most of the time most of us feel that we simply don't have enough time — "there's not enough hours in the day." Do we really think that if God upgraded the twenty-four-hour day to, let's say thirty, we'd really be happy with that? If we ain't makin it with the time we have, more time is not the answer. The answer lies in doin more with the time we have. This "more" factor is connected to the capacity we have for more love.

The end-of-time dimension of things unleashes more love so we can do and be more love, more of the time — gradually and eventually makin it be "all of the time," right up to the time when we slip out of time! See what I'm sayin? It's the "even as I have loved you" (Jn 13:34) in the new commandment of love Jesus gave us. Jesus loved us to the end; Jesus loved us even unto death, death on a Cross. How can we enter into this mode of being, this mode of lovin with the love with which we are loved? What can we do to have our way of thinkin and feelin change, with regard to our use of time so we don't waste any more time complainin that we don't have enough time? With JPII I say, "Do not be afraid to give your time to Christ! Yes, let us open our time to Christ, that he may cast light on it and give it direction. He is the one who knows the secret of time and the secret of eternity.... Time given to Christ is never time lost, but is time rather gained, so that our relationships and indeed our whole life may become more profoundly human."

▌et us open our time to Christ.

Today I would strongly urge everyone to rediscover Sunday: Do not be afraid to give your time to Christ! Yes, let us open our time to Christ, that he may cast light upon it and give it direction. He is the One who knows the secret of time and the secret of eternity, and he gives us "his day" as an ever new gift of his love. The rediscovery of this day is a grace which we must implore, not only so that we may live the demands of faith to the full, but also so that we may respond concretely to the deepest human yearnings. Time given to Christ is never time lost, but is rather time gained, so that our relationships and indeed our whole life may become more profoundly human.

— JPII, *Dies Domini* #7

St. Columban shows us how this "more" thing works with regard to love; more love more sufferin, more sufferin more healin, all because of more love: "The more a soul loves, the more it desires to love and the greater its suffering, the greater it healing."

Love restores and enriches love and heals all wounds. While there's some truth in the sayin "time heals all wounds," there's more truth in the fact of love healin all wounds and even usin wounds to heal, so great is this Love. Accordin to St. John of the Cross, "When God beholds the soul made attractive through grace, he is impelled to grant her more grace, for he dwells within her and is pleased with her.... Because this grace exalts, honors, and beautifies the soul in his sight, God loves her ineffably. He takes it even further and talks about the custom God has of giving more to whoever has more. And his gifts are multiplied in proportion to what the soul possesses" (*Magnificat*, November 2006, Vol. 8, No. 9, p. 355, 161).

So at the end of the day, "the end of time" has less to do with our dyin, and more to do with us livin — livin life to the full with the fullness of Love. This Love enriches us, in the words of Giusani, with "*the miracle of a man who becomes more man*" ("Traces," *Communion and Liberation International Magazine*, Vol. 8, No. 3, 2006, pp. 3-5). This "more" increases more and more until the end of time when the ineffable and immeasurable dimensions of love will definitively sweep us away into the infinite ocean of Love.

31. Love Alone

Love alone is the ultimate enrichment of our humanity and our world and the cultures of our world. Love alone can make us abound and increase in a way that is beneficial to everyone. Love alone can empower us to sustain an honest and consistent effort in workin for justice and practicin mercy, which is the formula for peace on a global level. This global level starts with you, your family, your friends, your neighborhood, the block, village, town, city, state, country, and nation! Love is the only power to pull all this together. As the great JPII said, "Ultimately it is love alone which succeeds in uprooting the tragic selfishness that lies deep within the human heart."

Culture is created through love.

It is precisely in this movement of self-transcendence, of recognition of the other, of the need to communicate with the other, that culture is created. But this drive to the other is only possible through love. Ultimately it is love alone which succeeds in uprooting the tragic selfishness that lies deep within the human heart. It is love which lies deep within the human heart. It is love which helps us to place others and the Other at the center of our lives.

— JPII, November 9, 1999, Address to the World of Culture

When we are most generous we are most living and most real.

We believe that the tendency to give, to share, to cherish, is the mainspring of the universe, ultimate cause of all that is, and reveals the Nature of God: and therefore that, when we are most generous we are most living and most real.... To enter the Divine order then, achieve the full life for which *we were made, means entering an existence which only has meaning as the channel and expression of an infinite, self-spending love.... When we look out towards this love that moves the stars and stirs in the child's heart and claims our total allegiance, and remember that this alone is Reality and we are only real so far as we conform to its demands, we see our human situation from a fresh angle.*

— EU, *Anthology*, pp. 42-43

The tendency of impoverished love is to reduce love to a need. Accordin to von B, "This would be the cynical destruction of love through selfishness.... Only in the acknowledgement of the pure grace of being loved can the lover also claim to be fulfilled by that love" (*Love Alone*, p. 54). EU affirms that "only love ... can embrace all human inconsistency and imperfection and see within it the stirring of the perfect." This ability of love to embrace all inconsistency and imperfection and see right there in the midst of these impoverishin energies the stirrings of the perfect of love, is somethin proper to the reality of love alone. Love alone provides the enrichin fullness to conquer and transform the effected and disorders of impoverished love. Love alone is capable of holdin this tension which is the basic foundational energy for peace in the world. JPII in his November 9, 1999 address to the World of Culture said, "Genuine culture respects the mystery of the human person, and must involve a dynamic exchange between the particular and the universal. It must seek a synthesis of unity and diversity. Love alone is capable of holding this tension in a creative and fruitful balance." Ultimately it is love alone, which succeeds in uprootin all the tragic selfishness that lies deep within the human heart. It is love alone, which is the fundamental vocation of every human person. It is love alone, which helps us to place others and the Other at the center of our lives.

Love can increase and abound.

May the Lord make you increase and abound in love for one another and for all men.

— Thessalonians 3:12

Love alone provides the enrichin fullness needed to heal the cultures and peoples of the world. B16 made this point clear in #39 of DCE — Love alone is the Light which energizes us to live with the courage necessary to shine in the darkness of the world; to keep on livin and workin — to keep on lovin: "Love is the light — and in the end, the only light — that can always illuminate a world grown dim and give us the courage needed to keep living and working." It is Love alone, as mercy, the great JPII tells us, that "is able to reach down into every human misery" (DM #6). And no matter how great the resistance we encounter against love, it is love alone that can have us surpass that resistance with a greater effort and determination because love is stronger than death.

The enrichin fullness of love is a great force deep in culture.

Love is like a great force hidden deep within cultures in order to urge them to overcome their incurable finiteness by opening themselves to him who is their Source and End, and to give them, when they do open themselves to his grace, enriching fullness.

— JPII, May 20, 1982, Letter Establishing the Pontifical Council for Culture

Strong resistance to love requires greater closeness to the mystery of Love.

No matter how strong the resistance of human history may be, no matter how marked the diversity of contemporary civilization, no matter how great the denial of God in the human world, so much greater must be the Church's closeness to that mystery which hidden for centuries in God, was then truly shared with man, in time through Jesus Christ.

— JPII, DM #15

32. The Victory of Love

When B16/Cardinal Ratzinger presided over the Holy Saturday Liturgy the week before the death of the great JPII, he referred to the victory of love that restores us to the original wholeness we had before the corruption of sin. The victory of love contained in the Resurrection of Jesus definitely defeats the dark and ugly powers of evil and makes us more beautiful than ever: *"This night is truly extraordinary, one in which the blazing light of the Risen Christ definitively defeats the dark power of evil and death, and rekindles hope and joy in the hearts of believers.... What was destroyed is rebuilt, what was aging is renewed and completely restored, more beautiful than ever, to its original wholeness."*

We are more than conquerors because of love.

Who shall separate us from the love of Christ? Shall tribulation, or distress, or persecution, or famine, or nakedness, or peril, or sword?... No, in all these things we are more than conquerors through him who loved us. For I am sure that neither death, nor life, nor angels, nor principalities, nor things present, nor things to come, nor powers, nor height, nor depth, nor anything else in all creation, will be able to separate us from the love of God in Christ Jesus our Lord.

— Romans 8:35, 37-38

In CCC 412, St. Thomas Aquinas alludes to the power of the victory of love unleashed in our lives that draws us always to greater good: "There is nothing to prevent human nature's being raised up to something greater, even after sin; God permits evil in order to draw forth some greater good" (St. Thomas Aquinas, *STh* III, 1, 3, *ad* 3; cf. *Rom* 5:20). In all things we are victorious through love, which makes us "more than conquerors" (Rom 8:37). In order to enrich love in the culture and the world, our capacity for love needs to be embraced and tapped. It's up to us, as JPII said at midnight Mass in 2001, to draw from the power of Jesus' victorious love *"by appropriating his logic of service and humility."* This is one of the ultimate lessons for us to learn somethin about love; to learn that I am loved by a Love that frees me in truth to have it be my greatest pleasure to give and to serve. The victory of love, in spite of every impoverishin factor in me, in the world, and the cultures of the world, makes me know deep in my heart, and makes me know way down deep into the depths of my soul and bones, that I am definitively loved by a great love. The victory of love makes me burn with a desire to want to love so great a love, a love that is ultimate, unconditional, and absolute. It is only with this love that we can be faithful and love to the end. This victory of love renews the world and the cultures of the world accordin to the designs of Love enablin all to reach fulfillment (cf. *Gaudium et Spes* #2).

The human being needs the victory of unconditional love.

It is not science that redeems man: man is redeemed by love. This applies even in terms of this present world. When someone has the experience of a great love in his life, this is a moment of "redemption" which gives a new meaning to his life. But soon he will also realize that the love bestowed upon him cannot by itself resolve the question of his life. It is a love that remains fragile. It can be destroyed by death. The human being needs unconditional love. He needs the certainty which makes him say: "neither death, nor life, nor angels, nor principalities, nor things present, nor things to come, nor powers, nor height, nor depth, nor anything else in all creation, will be able to separate us from the love of God in Christ Jesus our Lord" (Rom 8:38-39). If this absolute love exists, with its absolute certainty, then — only then — is man "redeemed," whatever should happen to him in his particular circumstances. This is what it means to say: Jesus Christ has "redeemed" us.

— B16, *Spe Salvi* #26

Signs of the victory of love are not easily seen due to the negative impact of the media and the culture of death, which affects both what we see and how we look. It's not that the signs of the victory of love aren't there, they're just hard to see.

Signs pointin to the victory are not lackin but are difficult to see.

In effect, signs which point to this victory are not lacking in our societies and cultures, strongly marked though they are by the "culture of death." It would therefore be to give a one-sided picture, which could lead to sterile discouragement, if the condemnation of the threats to life were not accompanied by the presentation of the positive signs at work in humanity's present situation. Unfortunately it is often hard to see and recognize these positive signs, perhaps also because they do not receive sufficient attention in the communications media. Yet, how many initiatives of help and support for people who are weak and defenseless have sprung up and continue to spring up in the Christian community and in civil society, at the local, national and international level, through the efforts of individuals, groups, movements and organizations of various kinds!

— JPII, EV #26

U got 2 pray (if you don't already have a copy, check out my second book, *U Got 2 Pray: 100 Prayers for Daily Living in Modern Culture*) in order burn with the victory of love. Through prayer, Love empowers us to be in communion with the victory of love in the world. JPII put it like this in his book *Crossing the Threshold of Hope* (pp. 25-26):

> *Through prayer God reveals himself above all as mercy —*
> *that is, Love that goes out to those who are suffering, Love*
> *that sustains, uplifts, and invites us to trust. The victory*
> *of good in the World is united originally with this truth. A*
> *person who prays professes such a truth and in a certain sense*
> *makes God, who is merciful Love present in the World.*

The victory of love is gonna help us learn somethin about love that's not easy. The victory of love in the Gospel helps us overcome fear and the bad feelings that come with it. This victory is far from some kind of easy mystical exaltation. CCC 643 helps us realize this truth: "Far from showing us a community seized by a mystical exaltation, the Gospels present us with disciples demoralized ('looking sad' [Lk 24:17, cf. Jn 20:19]) and frightened." In his excellent book of the poetry of JPII, Joseph Mauceri puts it like this: "The full business of this world is the triumph of love" (Joseph M. Mauceri, *The Fire of God, Forgiveness and Hope in the Poetry of John Paul II*, p. 18). Again, we see the same kind of thing with JPII in his 1994 *Letter to Families*. He challenges us to trust in the victory of love, to believe that love "*is really capable of triumphing over everything that is not love*" (#5).

Gandhi said somethin that reminds me of JPII (without the element of despair, which for JPII was transformed into hope through the Cross): "When I despair, I remember that all through history the way of truth and love has always won."

The ultimate expression of the truth of the victory of love that makes it possible for us to live in communion with love, so we can learn from the very heart of love somethin about love, is the fact of love makin itself noticed in our poverty, weakness, and sufferin. As JPII said in his encyclical *God Is Rich in Mercy* #3, this love is "an effective love, a love that addresses itself to man and embraces everything that makes up our humanity." This "everything" includes our impoverished love. "This love makes itself particularly noticed in contact with suffering, injustice, and poverty. In contact with the whole historical human condition which in various ways manifests man's limitation and frailty, both physical and moral." It is precisely here, in our weakness and brokenness, the moments when our love fails through our impoverished love, that the victory of love kicks in with its richness, the triumph of love with its victory in havin us learn somethin about love. As EU said, this victory of love "backs up our efforts by its grace coming into action just where our action fails" (EU, *Anthology*, pp. 70-71). Our sufferings are sweetened by love as we grow, through the great transformation, into the fullness of love with the love that is God.

The great transformation.

It is an unending and continuous transformation between falling and rising again, between the man of sin and the man of grace and justice. Mankind has made wonderful discoveries and achieved extraordinary results in the fields of science and technology. It has made great advances along the path of progress and civilization, and in recent times, one could say that it has succeeded in speeding up the pace of history. But the fundamental transformation, the one which can be called "original," constantly accompanies man's journey, and through all the events of history accompanies each and every individual. It is the transformation from "falling" to "rising," from death to life. It is also a challenge to people's consciences, a challenge to man's whole historical awareness. The challenge to follow the path of "not falling" in ways that are ever old and ever new, and of "rising again" if a fall has occurred.

— JPII, RM #52

Proclaim the victory of love in a world dominated by selfishness and hatred.

To God made man, who out of love accepted the most debasing punishment, multitudes of every race and culture now look. When their gaze is guided by the profound intuition of faith, they recognize in the Crucified One the unsurpassable "witness" of Love. From the Cross Jesus gathers into one people Jews and Gentiles, manifesting the will of his heavenly Father to make all mankind a single family gathered in his name. In the acute pain of the Suffering Servant we already hear the triumphant cry of the Risen Lord. Christ on the Cross is the King of the new people ransomed from the burden of sin and death. However twisted and confused the course of history may appear, we know that, by walking in the footsteps of the Crucified Nazarene, we shall attain the goal. Amid the conflicts of a world often dominated by selfishness and hatred, we, as believers, are called to proclaim the victory of Love.

— JPII, Good Friday, March 29, 2002

33. To the End

He loved them to the end.

Now before the festival of the Passover, Jesus knew that his hour had come to depart from this world and go to the Father. Having loved his own who were in the world, he loved them to the end.

— John 13:1

The Love that goes to the end is the Love, enriches our impoverished love, enablin us to love with the very love with which we are loved. It's the "as I have loved you" enrichment dimension of the Gospel of Jesus. Yes, there is a disastrously diminishin factor that is one of the root causes of all that impoverishes love, namely acceptin a "diminished Christ." When B16 went to Assisi on June 17, 2007, he said that it's not enough to come to Assisi to admire St. Francis. He continued, "Ever more often, Christians in our time find themselves facing the tendency to accept a diminished Christ, admired in His extraordinary humanity but rejected in the profound mystery of His divinity." The profound mystery of the divinity of Jesus is precisely the source by which he loved us "to the end."

It's only by lovin Jesus and imitatin him that we can transform history and make a mark on the culture with the love that goes to the end. On June 4, 2004, JPII spoke to the bishops from the United States, tellin them, "It is only by knowing, loving and imitating Christ that, with him, we can transform history by bringing Gospel values to bear in society and culture." There's always gonna be a tension between what is human and what is above and beyond the human. The necessity for transcendence finds an urgency precisely here, with the love that goes to the end, because there's no way we can continue to live day by day without bein carried by this love. "Love makes the Church live, and since it is eternal it makes her live forever, to the end of time" (B16, September 23, 2007).

Love is a mission, and the mission, like the love, is a mission that goes to the end. One of the many things I love about my community, the CFR's (The Community of Franciscan Friars of the Renewal, www.franciscanfriars.com), is that we have no "retirement." In other words, the mission of love goes literally "to the end." So we're not lookin at a fixed point, say like 65 or 75 years old to say, "You're retired, you're done." Nope, that's not the case with us. With us, we're done when we're done, literally. In other words, our mission is accomplished here on earth at "check out time"; our mission on earth is accomplished with death, our mission goes "to the end." Adrienne von Speyr says, "A mission is not something which can be fulfilled and completed once and for all. It is something alive and growing, something to be assumed daily, assented to daily" (*Handmaid of the Lord*, Ignatius Press, p. 47).

This kind of love that goes to the end involves endurance. Endurance is linked to the steadfast endurance and love of Jesus himself. In II Thessalonians 3:5, Paul prays for the hearts of the people to be directed by the Lord "to the love of God and to the steadfastness of Christ."

To share in the steadfastness of Christ.

To be steadfast means to stay firmly in place, not to be subject to change. The "steadfastness of Christ" St. Paul is talkin about in 2 Thess 3:5 is linked to endurance and fidelity, which are components of the love that goes "to the end." It's connected to God who is Love, who abides in "steadfast love" (Ex 34:7). On May 9, 1999, in his Angelus address, JPII directed these comments to a group from Romania: "I recall with reverence the witness borne during the persecution of so many Christians, both famous and unknown, who remained steadfast in the faith and continued to spread the Gospel, sometimes at the price of their own lives. This is the steadfastness of Christ, which makes us sharers in the love that goes to the end. This steadfast love is what held Mary up under the weight of the Cross to stand steadfast at the foot of the Cross."

This business about bein steadfast is a really big somethin to help us learn somethin about love. St. Cyprian, in his treatise on the Lord's Prayer, put it like this: "To love God with all one's heart; to love Him in that He is a Father; to fear Him in that He is God; to prefer nothing whatever to Christ, because He did not prefer anything to us; to remain steadfast in His love; to stand by His cross bravely and faithfully; when there is any contest on behalf of His name and honor, to show in words constancy in confessing our faith in Him; in torture, that confidence wherewith we do battle; in death, that patience whereby we are crowned — this is to desire to be fellow heirs with Christ; this is to do the commandment of God; this is to fulfill the will of the Father." Again, it's connected to Psalm 103:17, the steadfast love of the Lord is from everlasting to everlasting. This is the love that has no beginning and has no end, this is the love that carries us "to the end."

To learn somethin about love, more precisely to learn somethin about the love that goes "to the end," we got to learn somethin about trust and surrender. If u got 2 love, u got 2 trust; and if you're gonna trust, u got 2 surrender. Trust and surrender are two main components of love, which give birth to hope which holds us tight in the midst of all and every disappointment. B16 in SS #27 connects hope with love, precisely with the love that goes to the end: "Man's great, true hope which holds firm in spite of all disappointments can only be God — God who has loved us and who

continues to love us 'to the end,' until all 'is accomplished'
(cf. Jn 13:1 and 19:30)."

W̶hat we need in our love is the con– tinuous desire to love the One we love.

I want you all to fill your hearts with great love. Don't imagine that love, to be true and burning, must be extraordinary. No; what we need in our love is the continuous desire to love the One we love.... My soul may be in darkness. Trial and suffering are the surest test of my blind surrender. Surrender is also true love. The more we surrender, the more we love God and souls.

— Blessed Mother Teresa (from *Jesus the Word to Be Spoken*, St. Anthony Messenger Press, 1998, in *Magnificat*, August 2007, pp. 281-282, Vol. 9, No. 6)

On one of my many awesome mission trips to Uganda, I met an awesome Ugandan Little Sister of St. Francis, Sister Joan Babirye. I had the opportunity to spend some time with her. She is a holy veteran in the spirit of St. Francis for over fifty-five years and has spent many of those years sufferin intensely from physical issues with her legs, hip, and arms, and all this with great love and a great smile. She loved with the love that goes "to the end," and it was obvious.

At the time, I was workin on the book you are now readin. I was sharin with her how I did not want to come off as complainin about contemporary culture and criticize the many things about it that indeed need to be criticized. I was lookin for some help to prevent me from havin a narrow, puny point of view with regard to all the impoverished love stuff we've been looking at. Rather, I told her, I was hopin to expose the impoverishin energies and experiences of love and offer at least some kind of somethin for the enrichment of the love that is not loved. To offer some kind of help for us to learn somethin about love, about the love that goes "to the end." We both immediately turned to Francesco and recounted the event of St. Francis runnin through the streets of Assisi knockin door-to-door, burnin with love and shoutin out with the intensity of the urgency of love — as only he could do — "love is not loved."

Francesco burned with love for the love that was not loved, which was the love that goes to the end, the love which carried him to the end, the love that caused him to live and die with freedom and peace. "Man longs for love more than for freedom — freedom is the means and love the end" (Karol Wojtyla/JPII, *Love and Responsibility*, p. 136). To learn somethin about this love that goes "to the end" will never be complete until the end, because the education of the children of Love is never complete. As von B said, "The education of a child of God by the Holy Spirit is never completed" (von B, *Unless You Become Like This Child*, Ignatius Press, 1991).

And yes, this learnin somethin about love is never complete. Yet, this love that goes "to the end," this love alone that gives us the possibility of passionately pursuin and practicin love every day without ceasin, is present wherever this love is loved and wherever this love reaches us. Check out B16 in SS #31:

> *God is the foundation of hope: not any god, but the God who has a human face and who has loved us to the end, each one of us and humanity in its entirety. His Kingdom is not an imaginary hereafter, situated in a future that will never arrive; his Kingdom is present wherever he is loved and wherever his love reaches us. His love alone gives us the possibility of soberly persevering day by day, without*

ceasing to be spurred on by hope, in a world which by its very nature is imperfect. His love is at the same time our guarantee of the existence of what we only vaguely sense and which nevertheless, in our deepest self, we await: a life that is "truly" life.

Jesus leads us deeper into the mysteries of God/Love.

Amid our questions and difficulties and even our bitter disappointment, the Divine Wayfarer continues to walk at our side, opening to us the scriptures and leading us to a deeper understanding of the mysteries of God. When we meet Him fully we will pass from the light of the word to the light streaming from the Bread of Life. The Supreme fulfillment of His promise to "Be with us always" to the end of the age (Mt 28:20).

— JPII, MND #2

A mystery greater and deeper than our heart.

It seems as if the roots of evil lie deeper, as If evil contains a sort of mystery greater than man, one that transcends his history and his means of action.... It is difficult to measure the evil which is our lot on this earth. It is a mystery greater than man, deeper than his heart. Gethsemane and Calvary speak of it, and at the same time bear witness that in the history of man, in his heart, another mystery is at work, that of the redemption, which will work to the end to uproot evil.

— JPII, *Be Not Afraid*, pp. 84-85

Jesus helps us to learn somethin about the love that goes to the end by virtue of the fact and mystery of him stayin with us till the end of time. In this way, he helps us learn somethin about love by leadin us deeper into the mysteries of God, the mysteries of Love, in the midst of all our questions and difficulties. For the great JPII, the great mystery of the Redemption is the greatest help for us to learn somethin about love, the love that goes to the end. Quite often this lesson is difficult to learn because it seems as if the roots of evil are deeper than the roots of love. But this mystery of the Redemption which births the mystery of the love that goes to the end is bigger than all the evil combined in the history of evil; this mystery of love that goes to the end is bigger that human history and every heart that ever lived and will live; this mystery works to the end to uproot evil and establish the civilization of love burnin within us so we can burn ourselves out *on the altar of the Eucharist of history* as the great JPII did. Thus, we will come to know ourselves as bein so definitively loved, we will be able to embrace and carry "the burden of our greatness until the triumphant conclusion of our earthly trial" (Tadausz Styczen, Cardinal Stanislaw Dziwisz, *The Prayer of Gethsemane Goes On*, Lublin-Vaduz, pp. 26-27).

Tirelessly and with renewed intensity JPII lived the gospel of love that goes to the end.

In the first years of his pontificate, still young and full of energy, the Holy Father went to the very ends of the earth, guided by Christ. But afterward, he increasingly entered into the communion of Christ's sufferings; increasingly he understood the truth of the words: "Someone else will fasten a belt around you." And in the very communion with the suffering Lord, tirelessly and with renewed intensity, he proclaimed the Gospel, the mystery of that love which goes to the end (Jn 13:1).

— Cardinal Ratzinger/B16 at JPII's funeral

CONCLUSION

Buried under all the layers of all kinds of stuff is the preconditionin ... the pride and presumption of the beauty, truth, and goodness of the person. Love sees that beauty, truth, and goodness because love made it. Thus, the lifelong task for us is to be awakened by love — to have our eyes opened to see. This is the miracle of love that lends desirability and credibility to the appeal for us to surrender and submit to the demands of love. With this comes the gradual and real release and deliverance from all the refusals of the demands of love — deliverance and release from all evil because at the end of the day all evil in one way, shape, or form is a refusal of the demands of love. All the talk about the impoverishment of love was intended to stimulate your heart, soul, and mind for more love. It was an attempt to bend down over each occasion and instance of impoverished love, regardless of how seemingly insignificant, or whether it has catastrophic and global consequences, with the urgency of genuine love waiting for our response, givin what we need to respond.

If at any time, and for whatever reason, while your eyes have passed over the words printed on these pages which have passed through my mind, heart, and soul have in any way made you feel unloved, please forgive me and excuse me. I pray that every point and moment of tension encountered here will be a cause for an eternally conditioned enrichment of your encounter with love ... to make you feel restored to value. When we feel infinitely loved, there will be created in us the deepest sense of peace, which transcends our understandin, that will release us from the need to be fed by what we feel; then, the mysterious nature of this greatest of all gifts and mysteries will prepare us for the moment when darkness may hide the light of the love that conditioned us for the ultimate moment when we will fear nothing and have nothing to give except that naked crucified moment of nothing; in other words, that complete and total trustin surrender — shrouded in the darkness sustained by trust in the Love that carries us along, that Love for which the darkest of nights is as bright as day.

The goal: to love God with the perfection of love that only God can render unto Himself, so Jesus and the Holy Spirit and our transformation into love itself through, with, and in Him makes us new, radical, rebellious warriors of reckless love. One of the great helps in learnin somethin about love is boldness of faith, which JPII called "*mother of all miracles of love*" (JPII, May 3, 2004, Rimini).

To help us learn somethin about love that brings about a more complete response from deep within us that is rooted and grounded in love; to emerge from the ruins of impoverished love renewed and loved so lovingly and definitively that we contribute directly by participation in the dynamic progressive ever-expandin history of love at work in the heart of the world — love, the only reality and power that will stand till the end of time and keep us standin, waitin, and lovin for the completion of love's fulfillment, that "God may be everything to every one" (1 Cor 15:28), or in other words, that Love may be everything for everyone.

Who possesses God's love,
finds so much joy that every bitterness
transforms itself into sweetness,
and that every great weight becomes light.
One must not be astonished because living
in charity you live in God:
"God is love, and he who abides in love,
abides in God, and God abides in him" (1 Jn 4:16)....
Embrace, then, Jesus crucified, raising to Him
the eyes of your desire! Consider his burning love
*   for you,*
which made Jesus pour out His blood from every part
*   of His body!*
Embrace Jesus crucified, loving and beloved, and in Him
*   you will find*
true life because He is God made man. Let your heart
*   and your soul*
burn with the fire of love drawn from Jesus on the Cross!
You must, then, become love, looking at God's love
who loved you so much not because He had any
*   obligation towards you*
but out of pure gift, urged only by his ineffable love.
You will have no other desire than to follow Jesus!
As if you were drunken with love,
it will no longer matter
whether you are alone or in company:
do not think about many things,
but only about finding Jesus
and following Him!

— St. Catherine of Siena

THE LOVE ZONE

An Anthology of Love

The followin selection of texts are given here to be sources of inspiration for the empowerment of love in our lives helpin us to progress on the lifelong journey of learnin somethin about love. They come from a wide range of people. Not all of the passages use the word love or even talk directly about love. This goin beyond the linguistic presence of a word reinforces that love is most present and effective when lived. Yet all the passages presented are in one way or another related to and connected with love. Their presentation here is for us to read and reread them that as we learn somethin about love we will come to love learnin and thus live it well — maybe even to heroic proportions.

LZ 1

Tis better to have loved and lost
Than never to have loved at all.
— Alfred Lord Tennyson

LZ 2

Love turns work into rest.
— St. Teresa of Avila

LZ 3

The law of love is not concerned with what will be, what ought to be or what can be. Love does not reflect. It is unreasonable and knows no moderation.
— St. Peter Chrysologus

LZ 4

I always think that the best way to love God is to love many things.

— Vincent van Gogh (thinkexist.com)

LZ 5

I feel that there is nothing more artistic than to love people.

— Vincent van Gogh

LZ 6

Love many things, for therein lies the true strength, and whoever loves much performs much, and can accomplish much, and what is done in love is done well.

— Vincent van Gogh

LZ 7

God pays attention to our love. Not one of us is indispensable. God has the means to do all things and away with the work of the most capable human beings. We can work till we drop. We can work excessively. If what we do is not connected to love, our work is useless in God's eyes.

— Blessed Mother Teresa

LZ 8

God loves us the way we are, but too much to leave us that way.

— Leighton Ford (thinkexist.com)

LZ 9

Though our feelings come and go, God's love for us does not.

— C.S. Lewis

LZ 10

The most important thing in life is to learn how to give out love, and to let it come in.

— Morrie Schwartz

LZ 11

I have found the paradox, that if you love until it hurts, there can be no more hurt, only more love.
— Blessed Mother Teresa

LZ 12

There are four questions of value in life…. What is sacred? Of what is the spirit made? What is worth living for, and what is worth dying for? The answer to each is the same — only love.
— Johnny Depp

LZ 13

We say we love flowers, yet we pluck them. We say we love trees, yet we cut them down. And people still wonder why some are afraid when they are told they are loved.
— Anonymous (tx.com)

LZ 14

The one who loves you will make you weep.
— Argentinean Proverb

LZ 15

We cannot do great things on this earth, only small things with great love.
— Blessed Mother Teresa

LZ 16

Eventually you will come to understand that love heals everything, and love is all there is.
— Gary Zukay

LZ 17

Liberty is the measure of how much love we are capable of giving.
— Pope John Paul II (André Frossard, p. 90)

LZ 18

As long as one can admire and love, then one is forever young.
— Pablo Casals (dailycelebrations.com)

LZ 19

Where there is love there is life.
— Mahatma Gandhi (dailycelebrations.com)

LZ 20

Love never claims, it ever gives. Love ever suffers, never resents, never revenges itself.
— Mahatma Gandhi

LZ 21

Fear and love are contradictory terms. Love is reckless in giving away, oblivious as to what it gets in return. Love wrestles with the world as with the self and ultimately gains mastery over all other feelings. My daily experience, as of those who are working with me, is that every problem lends itself to solution if we are determined to make the law of truth and non-violence the law of life. For truth and non-violence are, to me, faces of the same coin. The law of love will work, just as the law of gravitation will work, whether we accept it or not. Just as a scientist will work wonders out of various applications of the law of nature, even so a man who applies the law of love with scientific precision can work greater wonders.
— Mahatma Gandhi (evelynrodriguez.typepad.com/
pointingtothemoon/2004/11/gandhi_on_love__1.html)

LZ 22

Where love is, there God is also.
— Mahatma Gandhi

LZ 23

I like your Christ, I do not like your Christians. Your Christians are so unlike your Christ.

— Mahatma Gandhi

LZ 24

Have we not come to such an impasse in the modern world that we must love our enemies — or else? The chain reaction of evil — hate begetting hate, wars producing more wars — must be broken, or else we shall be plunged into the dark abyss of annihilation.

— Martin Luther King, Jr.

LZ 25

I have decided to stick with love. Hate is too great a burden to bear.

— Martin Luther King, Jr.

LZ 26

It is not enough to say we must not wage war. It is necessary to love peace and sacrifice for it.

— Martin Luther King, Jr.

LZ 27

It may be true that the law cannot make a man love me, but it can keep him from lynching me, and I think that's pretty important.

— Martin Luther King, Jr.

LZ 28

Love is the only force capable of transforming an enemy into a friend.

— Martin Luther King, Jr.

LZ 29

A companion loves some agreeable qualities which a man may possess, but a friend loves the man himself.
— James Boswell (Scott Peck, *Abounding Grace: An Anthology of Wisdom*, Ariel Books, p. 273)

LZ 30

Love has nothing to do with what you are expecting to get — only what you are expecting to give — which is everything. What you will receive in return varies. But it really has no connection with what you give. You give because you love and cannot help giving. If you are very lucky, you may be loved back. That is delicious, but it does not necessarily happen.
— Katherine Hepburn, (S. Peck, *Abounding Grace*, p. 298)

LZ 31

Love talked about can be easily turned aside, but love demonstrated is irresistible.
— W. Stanley Mooneyham (S. Peck, *Abounding Grace*, p. 300)

LZ 32

Love and time are the only two things in this world that cannot be bought, only spent.
— Gary Jennings (S. Peck, *Abounding Grace*, p. 301)

LZ 33

Love your enemies, do good to those who hate you.
— Jesus (Luke 6:27)

LZ 34

The love of our neighbor in all its fullness simply means being able to say to him, "What are you going through?"
— Simone Weil (S. Peck, *Abounding Grace*, p. 102)

LZ 35

Love cannot remain by itself — it has no meaning. Love has to be put into action and that action is service.

 — Blessed Mother Teresa

LZ 36

Love is mercy's second name.

 — Pope John Paul II

LZ 37

Man is honored for his wisdom, loved for his kindness.

 — S. Cohen (S. Peck, *Abounding Grace*, p. 94)

LZ 38

Love is patient and kind.

 — St. Paul the Apostle (1 Corinthians 13:4)

LZ 39

If I have all faith, so as to remove mountains, but have not love, I am nothing.

 — St. Paul the Apostle (1 Corinthians 13:2)

LZ 40

He who knows himself knows everyone. He who can love himself, loves everyone.

 — Anthony of Egypt (*The Lion Christian Quotation Collection*, Hanna Ward, Jennifer Wild, A Lion Book, 1997)

LZ 41

Truth and love are wings that cannot be separated, for truth cannot fly without love, nor can love soar aloft without truth: their yoke is one of amity.

 — St. Ephrem the Syrian (*Lion*, p. 24)

LZ 42

The whole of human life is but a single day to those who labor with love.

— Gregory of Nazianzus (*Lion*, p. 27)

LZ 43

He who is filled with love is filled with God himself.

— St. Augustine of Hippo (*Lion*, p. 34)

LZ 44

For those who love, nothing is hard, and no task is too difficult if your desire is great.

— St. Jerome (*Lion*, p. 38)

LZ 45

Christ made love the stairway that would enable all Christians to climb up to heaven. So hold fast to love in all sincerity, give each other practical proof of it, and by your progress in it, make your ascent together.

— Fulgentius of Ruspe (*Lion*, p. 46)

LZ 46

Love's finest speech is without words.

— Hadewijch of Brabant, 13th C. Belgian mystic (*Lion*, p. 73)

LZ 47

A soul cannot live without loving. It must have something to love, for it was created to love.

— St. Catherine of Siena (*Lion*, p. 79)

LZ 48

Where there is no love, put love, and you will find love.

— St. John of the Cross

LZ 49

When the evening of our life comes, we shall be judged on Love.
— St. John of the Cross

LZ 50

The soul of one who loves God always swims in joy, always keeps holiday, and always is in a mood for singing.
— St. John of the Cross (*Lion*, p. 100)

LZ 51

It is not love in the abstract that counts. Men have loved brotherhood, the workers, the poor — but they have not loved personally. It is the hardest thing in the world to love.... It is never the brothers next to us, but the brothers in the abstract that are easy to love.
— Dorothy Day (*Lion*, p. 250)

LZ 52

Only love lasts forever. Alone, it constructs the shape of eternity in the earthly and shortlived dimensions of the history of man on the earth.
— Pope John Paul II (*Lion*, p. 272)

LZ 53

Love seeks only one thing: the good of the one loved. It leaves all the other secondary effects to take care of themselves. Love, therefore, is its own reward.
— Thomas Merton (*Lion*, p. 285)

LZ 54

Only through love can we attain communion with God.
— Albert Schweitzer (*Lion*, p. 308)

LZ 55

Love is self-sufficient; it is pleasing to itself, and on its own account. Love is its own payment, its own reward.
— St. Bernard of Clairvaux (*Lion*, p. 62)

LZ 56

Love counters power, and the divine affirms the human being's capacity for freedom, an irreducible capacity for perfection, for attaining happiness — for meeting the Other, God. The divine is love, as this splendid poem by Tagore witnesses:

> *By all means they try to hold me secure who love me in this world.*

> *But it is otherwise with thy love which is greater than theirs, and they keepest me free. Lest I forget them they never venture to leave me alone. But day passes after day, and thou are not seen. If I call thee not in my prayers, if I keep not thee in my heart, thy love for me still waits for my love.*
— Luigi Giussani, *The Religious Sense*, p.93

LZ 57

Love is the divine vitality that everywhere produces and restores life. To each and every one of us, it gives the power of working miracles if we will.
— Lydia Maria Child (*Lion*, p. 168)

LZ 58

God is love, and in the saints the Holy Spirit is love. Dwelling in the Holy Spirit, the saints behold hell and embrace it too in their love.
— Staretz Silouan (*Lion*, p. 217)

LZ 59

Christian love is not the world's last word about itself — it is God's final word about himself, and so about the world.
— von B (*Lion*, p. 229)

LZ 60

Let the love of God be stronger than death in you.
— John of Apamea (*Lion*, p. 40)

LZ 61

Love him totally who gave himself totally for your love.
— St. Clare of Assisi (*Lion*, p. 71)

LZ 62

To love God you need three hearts in one — a heart of fire for him, a heart of flesh for your neighbor, and a heart of bronze for yourself.
— St. Benedict Joseph Labré (*Lion*, p. 150)

LZ 63

It is always springtime in the heart that loves God.
— St. Jean Baptiste Marie Vianney (*Lion*, p. 196)

LZ 64

Love makes the whole difference between an execution and martyrdom.
— Evelyn Underhill (*Lion*, p. 220)

LZ 65

Mysticism is the name of that organic process which involves the perfect consummation of the love of God.
— Evelyn Underhill (*Lion*, p. 22)

LZ 66

A saint is a human creature devoured and transformed by love: a love that has dissolved and burnt out these instinctive passions, acquisitive and combative, proud and greedy, which commonly rule the lives of men.
— Evelyn Underhill

LZ 67

The nearer we draw to God in our love for him, the more we are united together by our love for our neighbor; and the greater our union with our neighbor, the greater is our union with God.
— Dororheus of Gaza (*Lion*, p. 46)

LZ 68

He alone loves the Creator perfectly who manifests a pure love for his neighbor.
— Bede (*Lion*, p. 54)

LZ 69

We can find no greater inspiration to love even our enemies as brothers and sisters — as we must if our love is to be perfect — than grateful remembrance of Christ's wonderful patience.
— Aelred of Rievaulx (*Lion*, p. 62)

LZ 70

It is profitless to fuss over human statutes and neglect the command of God which bids us love our neighbor as ourselves — on which St. Augustine teaches that "neighbor" must be taken to mean everybody.
— Robert Kilwardby (*Lion*, p. 75)

LZ 71

You can never love your neighbor without loving God.
— Jacques Benigne Bossuet (*Lion*, p. 114)

LZ 72

The love of our neighbor is the only door out of the dungeon of the self.
— George MacDonald (*Lion*, p. 180)

LZ 73

Give me such love for God and men as will blot out all hatred and bitterness.
— Dietrich Bonhoeffer

LZ 74

The Lord bestows such grace on his chosen that they embrace the whole earth, the whole world, with their love, and their souls burn with longing that all should be saved and behold the glory of the Lord. Blessed is the soul that loved her brother, for our brother is our life.
— Staretz Silouan

LZ 75

Love of God is the root, love of our neighbor is the fruit of the Tree of Life. Neither can exist without the other, but the one is cause and the other effect.
— William Temple

LZ 76

Christianity is a person, one who loved us so much, one who calls for our love.
— Archbishop Oscar Romero

LZ 77

Even when I'm old and grey, I won't be able to play it, but I'll still love the game.
— Michael Jordan

LZ 78

The saints' burning love is the explanation of how and why they exult vastly more in creation and in its Author than the lesser of us do.
— Thomas Dubay

LZ 79

You cannot love a car the way you love a horse. The horse brings out human feelings the way machines cannot do. Things, like machines, may develop or neglect certain things in people.... Machines make our life impersonal and stultify certain elements in us and create an impersonal environment.
— Albert Einstein

LZ 80

We are not enemies, but friends. We must not be enemies. Though passion may have strained it must not break our bonds of affection. The mystic chords of memory, stretching from every battlefield and patriot grave to every living heart and hearthstone all over this broad land, will yet swell the chorus of the Union, when again touched, as surely they will be, by the better angels of our nature.
— Abraham Lincoln (First Inaugural Address, March 4, 1861)

LZ 81

Gravitation is not responsible for people falling in love.
— Albert Einstein

LZ 82

A religious man is a person who holds God and man in one thought at one time, at all times, who suffers harm done to others, whose greatest passion is compassion, whose greatest strength is love and defiance of despair.
— Abraham Joshua Heschel

LZ 83

A test of a people is how it behaves toward the old. It is easy to love children. Even tyrants and dictators make a point of being fond of children. But the affection and care for the old, the incurable, the helpless are the true gold mines of a culture.
— Abraham Joshua Heschel

LZ 84

A joyful heart is the normal result of a heart burning with love.
— Blessed Mother Teresa

LZ 85

In love all things are shared, and so if you love Jesus,
everything of his is yours.
— *The Cloud of Unknowing*

LZ 86

I have called you friends, for all that I have heard from my
Father I have made known to you.
— Jesus (John 15:15)

LZ 87

Though we sin continually, he loves us endlessly, and so gently
does he show us our sin that we repent of it quietly, turning our
mind to the contemplation of his mercy, clinging to his love and
goodness, knowing that he is our cure, understanding that we
do nothing but sin.
— Julian of Norwich

LZ 88

If there is on earth anywhere a lover of God who is always kept
safe from falling, I know nothing of it — for it was not shown
me. But this was shown: that in falling and rising again we are
always held close in one love.
— Julian of Norwich

LZ 89

Love is not a stoic act of will in which one heroically overlooks
the nastiness of the other. I do not look at the bad news in the
other, noting all of his weak and irritating features, and then
say, "It is my Christian duty to love that irritating, boorish,

weak, and inferior thing. Therefore, I will, I will, I really will!"
Clearly enough, there is no love in that.
— Robert J. Spitze

LZ 90

The mystics, to give them their short familiar name, are men
and women who insist that they know for certain the presence
and activity of that which they call the Love of God.
— Evelyn Underhill

LZ 91

Love without service and sacrifice is an impossibility.
— Evelyn Underhill

LZ 92

There is a sacredness in tears. They are not the mark of
weakness, but of power. They speak more eloquently than ten
thousand tongues. They are messengers of overwhelming grief
and unspeakable love.
— Washington Irving

LZ 93

Love cannot rest [either for good or evil]. What is it in each
person that works not only for good but for evil, if not love?
Crimes, adulteries, disgraces, murders, incontinence of all
sorts: Is it not love that brings them all about? Purify your love,
then re-channel the water that flows into the sewer so that it
will flow into the garden!
— St. Augustine (*On Psalm 31*)

LZ 94

It is only when we look the Crucified One in the eye that we
recognize the abyss of selfishness — even that which we have
been accustomed to call love.
— von B

LZ 95

In every situation think more about loving than working.
— St. Maximilian Kolbe

LZ 96

O Divine Jesus, engrave in my heart the love of your cross and let me imitate that love of your Cross.
— St. Bernadette

LZ 97

Reason speaks in words alone. But love has a song.
— Joseph de Maistre

LZ 98

Only he who loves can sing.
— St. Augustine

LZ 99

There is more in love than people generally suppose.
— Vincent van Gogh

LZ 100

Everyone is sent into this world with the sole purpose of loving other people.
— Leo Tolstoy

LZ 101

The only perfection which is necessary is perfection of love ... that is why we came into this world.
— Leo Tolstoy

LZ 102

We cannot but love the beautiful.
— St. Augustine

LZ 103

A man who has discovered a great love feels really rich and knows that this is the true pearl, that this is the treasure of his life and not all the other things he may possess.
— Pope Benedict XVI, March 2, 2007

LZ 104

Of all forms of caution, caution in love is the most fatal.
— Anonymous

LZ 105

I long to see you set afire, swallowed up and consumed in his blazing charity, for we know that those who are set afire and consumed in that charity loathe all self-consciousness. That is what I want you to do. I am inviting you, in this blazing charity, to plunge into a peaceful sea, a deep sea. I have just rediscovered the sea — not that the sea is new, but it's new to me in the way my soul experiences it — in the words, "God is love."… These words echo within me that everything that is done is simply love, because everything is made entirely of love. This is why he says, "I am God, Love." This sheds light on the priceless mystery of the Incarnate Word, who out of sheer love was given in such humility that it confounds my pride. It teaches us to look not at just what he did, but at the blazing love this word has given us. It says that we should do as a loving person does when a friend comes with a gift; not looking at the friend's hands to see what the gift is, but looking with the eyes of love at the friend's loving heart. And this is what God's supreme, eternal, more tender than tender goodness wants us to do when he visits our soul. So when he comes to you with his incalculable blessings, let your memory open up at once to receive what your understanding has seen in his divine love, and let your will rise up in blazing desire to receive and gaze upon the burning heart of the giver, the good gentle Jesus. In this way you will find yourself swallowed up and clothed in the

fiery gift of the blood of God's son. And you will be freed from all suffering and grief.
— St. Catherine of Sienna

LZ 106

A bell is no bell till you ring it,
A song is no song till you sing it,
And love in your heart
Wasn't put there to stay —
Love isn't love
Till you give it away.
— Oscar Hammerstein, *Sound of Music*, "You Are Sixteen" (reprise)

LZ 107

"Suffering man belongs to us," said my unforgettable predecessor John Paul II.... Jesus loves us and teaches us to love, he challenges us to love.
— Pope Benedict XVI

LZ 108

Prayer can progress, as a genuine dialogue of love, to the point of rendering the person wholly possessed by the divine Beloved, vibrating at the Spirit's touch, resting filially within the Fathers heart.... It is a journey totally sustained by grace, which nonetheless demands an intense spiritual commitment and is no stranger to painful purifications.... But it leads, in various possible ways, to the ineffable joy experienced by the mystics as "nuptial union."
— Pope John Paul II, NMI #33

LZ 109

Love is like a friendship caught on fire. In the beginning a flame, very pretty, often hot and fierce, but still only light and

flickering. As love grows older, our hearts mature and our love becomes as coals, deep-burning and unquenchable.
— Bruce Lee

LZ 110

He felt that he was not simply close to her, but that he did not know where he ended and she began.
— Leo Tolstoy

LZ 111

Love never reasons but profusely gives; gives, like a thoughtless prodigal, its all, and trembles lest it has done too little.
— Hannah Moore

LZ 112

The love game is never called off on account of darkness.
— Tom Masson

LZ 113

A man is not where he lives but where he loves.
— A Latin proverb

LZ 114

The belief that love can reach into the afterlife, that reciprocal giving and receiving is possible, in which our affection for one another continues beyond the limits of death — this has been a fundamental conviction of Christianity throughout the ages and it remains a source of comfort today. Who would not feel the need to convey to their departed loved ones a sign of kindness, a gesture of gratitude, or even a request for pardon?
— Pope Benedict XVI, *Spe Salvi* #48

LZ 115

Love in action is a harsh and dreadful thing compared with love in dreams.
— Fyodor Dostoevski

LZ 116

You can give without loving, but you can never love without giving.
— Author Unknown

LZ 117

Love is the greatest refreshment in life.
— Pablo Picasso

LZ 118

Light means knowledge; it means truth, as contrasted with the darkness of falsehood and ignorance. Light gives us life, it shows us the way. But light, as a source of heat, also means love. Where there is love, light shines forth in the world; where there is hatred, the world remains in darkness.
— Pope Benedict XVI, December 24, 2005

LZ 119

Love enables us to see things that those who are without love cannot see.
— Thich Nhat Nanh

LZ 120

I am definitively loved, and whatever happens to me — I am awaited by this Love. And so my life is good.
— St. Josephine Bakhita

LZ 121

Love can be a collision in which two selves realize profoundly they ought to belong to each other even though they have no convenient moods and sensations. It is one of these processes in the universe which bring a synthesis, unite what was divided, broaden and enrich what was limited and narrow.
— Karol Wojtyla/John Paul II, *The Jeweler Shop*

LZ 122

In love did God bring the world into existence; in love is God going to bring it to that wondrous transformed state, and in love will the world be swallowed up in the great mystery of the One who has performed all these things; in love will the whole course of the governance of creation be finally comprised.
— St. Isaac of Syria

LZ 123

No one is born hating another person because of the color of his skin, or his background, or his religion. People must learn to hate, and if they can learn to hate, they can be taught to love, for love comes more naturally to the human heart than its opposite.
— Nelson Mandela

LZ 124

There are more love songs than anything else. If songs could make you do something, we'd all love one another.
— Frank Zappa

LZ 125

Get not your friends by bare compliments, but by giving them sensible tokens of your love.
— Socrates

LZ 126

I still believe that all you need is love.
— John Lennon

LZ 127

Whenever you are confronted with an opponent, conquer him with love.
— Mahatma Gandhi

LZ 128

We have to love until it hurts. It is not enough to say, "I love."
We must put that love into a living action. And how do we do
that? By giving until it hurts.... True love causes pain. Jesus in
order to give us the proof of his love, died on the Cross. A mother
in order to give birth to her baby has to suffer. If you really love
one another, you will not be able to avoid making sacrifices.
— Blessed Mother Teresa

LZ 129

The person who lives in love reaps the fruit of life from God,
and while yet in this world, even now breathes the air of the
Resurrection.
— St. Isaac of Syria

LZ 130

Won over by your useless efforts, he will come down himself,
and taking you in his arms, he will carry you.
— St. Thérèse of Lisieux

LZ 131

Liking or affection is primarily a feeling; love is a matter of
decision or action.
— Scott Peck, *Abounding Grace*

LZ 132

Go on loving me like this, I need a great deal of love in order to
live and I know that I have to love "as not loving," in St. Paul's
sense, and beyond St. Paul's sense. What a terrible vocation!
It is for this that God has your marvelous love at my side....
But Jacques, to live like this is a martyrdom, it is no longer to
have anywhere to lay one's head.... What is wonderful is that
I can take this rest in your heart without in any way hindering
Christ's action in us. God is so much with you. And you are
truly my only sweetness in this world.
— Raissa Maritain

LZ 133

A person who does not tolerate suspicion or disparagement (= a person who does not tolerate suspicion or disparagement of others) possesses true love.
— Philokalia, Vol. II, p. 307

LZ 134

When the love of Jesus is kindled and burns in the souls of the saints, it imprints in their hearts the new things of heaven.
— St. Isaac, The Book of Grace

LZ 135

Implant in me the astringent (= increase) of Thy love, that by being drawn away by fervent love for Thee, I may come forth from this world. Awake in me understanding of the humility, wherewith Thou didst sojourn in the world in the tenement composed of our members which by the mediation of the Holy virgin Thou didst bear, that with this continual and unfailing recollection, I may accept the humility of my nature with delight.
— St. Isaac of Syria

LZ 136

Let us not tire of preaching love, it is the force that will overcome the world. Let us not tire of preaching love. Though we see that waves of violence succeed in drowning the fire of Christian love, love must win out, it is the only thing that can.
— Archbishop Oscar Romero, November 20, 1977

LZ 137

The "yes" of Jesus and Mary is thus renewed in the "yes" of the saints, especially martyrs who are killed because of the Gospel. I stress this because yesterday, March 24, the anniversary of the assassination of Archbishop Oscar Romero of San Salvador, we celebrated the Day of Prayer and Fasting for Missionary

Martyrs: Bishops, priests, Religious and lay people struck down while carrying out their mission of evangelization and human promotion. These missionary martyrs, as this year's theme says, are the "hope of the world," because they bear witness that Christ's love is stronger than violence and hatred. They did not seek martyrdom, but they were ready to give their lives in order to remain faithful to the Gospel. Christian martyrdom is only justified when it is a supreme act of love for God and our brethren.

— B16, Angelus, March 25, 2007

LZ 138

It is obviously impossible to love all men in any strict and true sense. What is meant by loving all men is to feel well-disposed to all men, to be ready to assist them, and to act toward those who come in our way as if we loved them. We cannot love those about whom we know nothing; except indeed we view them in Christ, as the object of His Atonement, that is, rather in faith than in love. And love, besides, is a habit, and cannot be obtained without actual practice, which on so large a scale is impossible. We see then how absurd it is when writers (as is the manner of some who slight the Gospel) talk magnificently about loving the whole human race with a comprehensive affection, of being the friends of all mankind, and the like. Such vaunting professions, what do they mean? That such men have certain benevolent feelings towards the world — feelings and nothing more, nothing more than unstable feelings, the mere offspring of an indulged imagination, which exists only when their minds are wrought upon, and are sure to fail them in their hour of need. This is not to love men, it is but to talk about love. The real love of man must depend on practice, and therefore, must begin by exercising itself on our friends around us, otherwise it will have no existence. By trying to love our relations and friends, by submitting to their wishes, though contrary to our own, by bearing with their infirmities, by overcoming their occasional waywardness by kindness, by

*dwelling on their excellences, and trying to copy them, thus
it is that we form in our hearts that root of charity, which,
though small at first, may, like the mustard seed, at lease even
overshadow the earth.*
— St. John Newman

LZ 139

*So this morning, as I look into your eyes and into the eyes of all
my brothers in Alabama and all over America and all over the
world, I say to you: "I love you. I would rather die than hate
you."*
— Martin Luther King, Jr. (November 17, 1957,
Dexter Ave. Baptist Church)

LZ 140

*Love profits in its practice. I love because I love; I love that I
may love.*
— St. Bernard of Clairvaux

LZ 141

*Those who have not accustomed themselves to love their
neighbors, whom they have seen, will have nothing to lose or
gain, nothing to grieve at or rejoice in, in their larger plans
of benevolence. They will take no interest in them for their
own sake; rather they will engage in them, because experience
demands, or credit is gained, of an excuse found for being busy.*
— Cardinal Newman

LZ 142

*No one who is in love with himself is capable of loving God.
The man who loves God is the one who mortifies his self-love
for the sake of the immeasurable blessings of Divine Love....
Anyone alive to the love of God can be recognized from the
way he constantly strives to glorify him by fulfilling all his
commandments and by delighting in his own abasement....*

I know a man, though lamenting his failure to love God as much as he desires, yet loves him so much that his soul burns with ceaseless longing for God to be glorified, and for his own complete effacement.... He fulfills his priestly duty by celebrating the Liturgy, but his intense love for God is an abyss that swallows up all consciousness of his high office.... Anyone who loves God in the depths of his heart has already been loved by God. In fact, the measure of a man's love for God depends upon how deeply aware he is of God's love for him. When this awareness is keen, it makes whoever possesses it long to be enlightened by the divine light, and this longing is so intense that it seems to penetrate his very bones. He loses all consciousness of himself and is entirely transformed by the love of God.... Once the love of God has released him from self-love, the flame of Divine Love never ceases to burn in his heart and he remains united to God by an irresistible longing.

— Diadochus of Photice

LZ 143

Christianity "is a creator of culture in its very foundation" (Speech to UNESCO, June 2, 1980, n. 10; L'Osservatore Romano English Edition, June 23, 1980, p. 10). In the Christian world, a truly prestigious culture has flourished throughout the centuries, as much in the area of literature and philosophy as in the sciences and the arts. The very concept of beauty in ancient Europe is largely the result of the Christian culture of its peoples, and its landscape reflects this inspiration. The center around which this culture has developed is the heart of our faith, the Eucharistic mystery. Cathedrals, humble country churches, religious music, architecture, sculpture, and painting all radiate the mystery of the verum Corpus natum de Maria Virgine, *towards which everything converges in a movement of wonder. As for music, I am glad to commemorate Giovanni Pierluigi da Palestrina this year, on the occasion of the fourth centenary of his death. It would seem that, after a troubled period, the Church regained a voice made peaceful* through contemplation of the Eucharistic mystery, like the calm breathing of a soul that knows it is loved by God.

Christian culture admirably reflects man's relationship with God, made new in the redemption. It opens us to the contemplation of the Lord, true God and true man. This culture is enhanced by the love that Christ pours into our hearts (cf. Rom 5:5) and by the experience of disciples called to emulate their Master. Such sources have given rise to an intense awareness of the meaning of life, a strength of character that blossoms in the heart of Christian families, and a sense of finesse unknown in the past. Grace awakens, frees, purifies, orders, and expands the creative powers of man. While it invites asceticism and renunciation, it does so in order to free the heart, a freedom eminently conducive to artistic creation as well as to thought and action based on truth.

In this culture, therefore, the influence of the saints is decisive: through the light that they emanate through their inner freedom, through the power of their personality, they have made a mark on the artistic thought and expression of entire periods of our history. It is enough to mention St. Francis of Assisi. He had a poet's temperament, something which is amply confirmed by his words, his attitude, his innate sense of symbolic gesture. Although his concerns were far removed from the world of literature, he was, nevertheless, the creator of a new culture, both in thought and in art. A St. Bonaventure or a Giotto could not have developed had it not been for him.

— Pope John Paul II to the Pontifical Council for Culture, March 18, 1994, #8-9

More titles
from Father Stan

U Got 2 Pray
978-1-93170-996-5 (ID# T53),
Paperback, 256 pp., $9.95

Original, relevant, teen-friendly
prayers deliver the positive influence
to rise above the mainstream and
develop a rock-solid spirit. Filled with
relevant Scripture passages, real-life
examples, and the one-of-a-kind
energy of Father Stan.

U Got 2 Believe!
978-0-87973-911-9 (ID# 911),
Paperback, 224 pp., $12.95

Written in their language and on their
terms, this energetic book educates
and inspires teens, helping them find
the power that's available to them.
What R U waiting for?

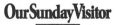

Our Sunday Visitor

Bringing Your Catholic Faith to Life

Call 800.348.2440 to order or visit us at www.osv.com